MEDIATION REFRAMING: LIFE AND PEACE FROM DEATH AND WAR

How words and language bring you life and peace

David Hoicka

I am grateful for the kindness over the years of the following:

1. Singapore State Courts and its several branches, which have provided me with seemingly endless opportunities to mediate, along with many other branches of the Singapore Government.

2. Singapore Mediation Centre, where I am one of the Principal Mediators, Mediation Coaches, and Mediation Assessors.

3. New York State Courts, in particular South Bronx, Brooklyn and Manhattan, which also provided me with seemingly endless opportunities to work with real people and their very important life problems

In addition I thank Vasilyeva of YayImages.com for the excellent image which brings life, emotion, and happiness to my book. May your life have the same happiness and love which your image expresses.

David Hoicka
Singapore Mediation Solutions
Singapore

CONTENTS

Title Page

Dedication

Introduction

Why Translate Idioms and Phrases   1

1. Cultivating a culture of life, peace, happiness, and mutual friendship   3

2. Reframing helps humans at all levels find peace and happiness.   7

3. More than 700 Idioms and Phrases Reframed for Life and Peace   11

INTRODUCTION

In this guide, I've gathered over 700 English idioms and phrases that touch on the emotions, feelings, and dreams linked to death and the harsh realities of war and conflict. My goal is to let you, the reader, see for yourself the widespread and deep-rooted presence of death-related imagery in our culture and society.

It's a truth that everyone's journey ends in death, but it's equally important to remember that we are all living right now. Through this work, I aim to shift the focus from death to life for all these expressions (sometimes offering more than one way to see an idiom or phrase differently). This way, I show numerous paths to view life instead of death, peace instead of war, friendship instead of conflict, and hope instead of despair.

I've organized the idioms alphabetically in English and assigned each a number. For those reading in another language, I've maintained the same numbered sequence to make it easier to cross-reference.

As you explore the idioms and the various new perspectives I present, it's enlightening to notice how many of these phrases slip into our everyday language and shape our view of the world, often without us even realizing it.

By simply flipping through and reflecting on these sayings,

you'll find dozens, if not hundreds, that when reinterpreted, can infuse life, hope, peace, and happiness into our conversations and thoughts.

If this collection of emotional transformations can save even one life or bring happiness to a single person, it will fill me also with hope and happiness, knowing I've made a difference as the author.

I wish you peace, happiness, good health and prosperity always.

David Hoicka
Singapore Mediation Solutions
Singapore

Why Translate Idioms And Phrases

Idioms are a shortcut to big feelings. They help us talk about things that are hard to say, like how we feel when someone dies in a war. Even though idioms are different in every language, the feelings they talk about are pretty much the same for everyone. That's why translating them can help people from different places, like Ukraine and Russia, see that they're not so different after all.

Finding The Right Words

Sometimes, there's no perfect match for an idiom in another language. That's when translators have to get creative. They might find a different idiom that has a similar feeling, or they might explain the idea in a new way. The goal is to keep the meaning and the emotion, so people can connect, even if they're using different words. Even though idioms can be really different across languages, they often show that we all feel similar things. People everywhere understand the pain of loss and the hope for peace.

Reframing To Find Our Happiness And Peace

In this collection, I've brought together over 700 sayings that, even when they're not perfectly translated, show us how common talk of death and loss is in all languages and cultures. That's why it's so important to change the way we talk about these things in every language—to bring back our natural feelings of life, hope, joy, and peace. Even if it's not perfect, changing the way we translate these sayings can help us understand our deep, often hidden feelings of hurt and loss. I really hope that these new ways of expressing old sayings will help us see past the death-related images that often control how we feel and stop us from being happy. By changing our words, no matter what language we speak, we can start to live better lives filled with friendship and success.

Bridges For Shared Experiences

Translating idioms about death and dying in war isn't just about language. It's about finding the shared human experiences in those words. It's a way to help people from different cultures, like in Ukraine and Russia, understand each other a little better. And when people understand each other, they have a better chance of finding peace and building a future where everyone can be happy and healthy. That's the power of translation – it turns words into bridges that can bring us all a little closer together.

I wish you peace, happiness, good health and prosperity always.

David Hoicka
Singapore Mediation Solutions
Singapore

1. Cultivating A Culture Of Life, Peace, Happiness, And Mutual Friendship

In our world today, the imagery of death often casts a long shadow over our cultural landscapes. From the stories we tell to the news that headlines our days, it's not uncommon to find ourselves enveloped in narratives that focus on the darker aspects of human existence. However, there's a growing movement that seeks to shift this focus, to replace the pervasive imagery of death with symbols of life, peace, happiness, good health, mutual cooperation, respect, and prosperity. This essay explores the importance of this shift and how it can transform our collective consciousness and societal structures.

The Power Of Imagery

Imagery, in its essence, is a powerful tool that shapes our perceptions, emotions, and actions. When our cultural narratives are dominated by images of conflict, suffering, and demise, it can skew our worldview towards pessimism and despair. This constant exposure can desensitize us to the value of life and the potential for positive change. Conversely, when we surround ourselves with imagery that celebrates life and its myriad possibilities, we open our hearts and minds to hope, joy, and the infinite capacity for human kindness and innovation.

Cultivating A Culture Of Life

The first step in cultivating a culture that prioritizes life-affirming imagery is to recognize the impact of our current cultural narratives. By acknowledging the ways in which death-centric imagery influences our attitudes and behaviors, we can begin to consciously choose alternatives that uplift and inspire. This doesn't mean ignoring the realities of pain and suffering but rather balancing our awareness with equal attention to stories of resilience, recovery, and mutual aid.

Promoting Peace And Happiness

Peace and happiness are not merely personal aspirations; they are collective goals that can guide the development of our societies. By integrating symbols of peace in our public spaces, media, and art, we encourage a mindset that looks for resolution rather than conflict. Similarly, by celebrating moments of joy and contentment in our daily lives, we reinforce the idea that happiness is not a fleeting state but a sustainable one, achievable through community support and personal well-being.

Good Health As A Common Good

Good health is a fundamental right and a cornerstone of a prosperous society. When our cultural imagery emphasizes the importance of physical, mental, and emotional well-being, it encourages policies and practices that prioritize healthcare, mental health resources, and holistic approaches to wellness. This shift in focus from illness to wellness invites us to imagine a world where everyone has access to the care and support they need to thrive.

Mutual Cooperation And Respect

At the heart of a life-affirming culture is the principle of mutual cooperation and respect. This means moving beyond tolerance to a deep appreciation of our differences and an active engagement in building bridges between diverse communities. By highlighting stories of collaboration and respect, we model the kind of social fabric that is resilient in the face of challenges and enriched by its diversity.

Prosperity For All

Finally, replacing the imagery of death with that of life means envisioning a world where prosperity is shared. It's about creating economies that serve the well-being of all people, not just a privileged few. Through cultural narratives that emphasize fairness, sustainability, and innovation, we can inspire actions that lead to a more equitable distribution of resources and opportunities.

Envisioning Peace Amidst Conflict

The ongoing conflict between Ukraine and Russia serves as a stark reminder of the devastating impact of war on human lives and societies. Yet, within this context lies the opportunity to reframe our perspectives and envision a future marked by peace and mutual understanding. Drawing from the works of psychologist Alice Miller, we recognize how past traumas, including those inflicted by war, shape our lives both consciously and unconsciously. By acknowledging these traumas and working towards healing, societies can pave the way for genuine peace and reconciliation.

Celebrating Life

The imagery we choose to surround ourselves with has profound implications for our individual and collective futures. By consciously shifting our focus from death to life, we can cultivate a culture that values peace, happiness, health, cooperation, respect, and prosperity. This transformation requires the participation of everyone, from senior management to individuals in every community. Together, we can create a world that celebrates life in all its forms, a world where every person has the opportunity to live fully and contribute to the common good.

2. Reframing Helps Humans At All Levels Find Peace And Happiness.

The transformative power of reframing helps navigate complex international disputes as well as local business and family issues. This is because at all levels, we are all human beings generally with similar basic emotional and physical goals and needs. This essay delves into the essence of reframing in mediation, exploring its potential to foster peace, happiness, good health, mutual cooperation, respect, and prosperity, especially in the face of adversity.

Understanding Reframing In Mediation

At its core, reframing is a mediation technique that involves altering the perspective on a conflict or problem to open new avenues for understanding and solution-finding. It's about shifting the dialogue from a negative, often confrontational stance, to a positive, collaborative one. In the context of the ongoing conflict between Ukraine and Russia, reframing could mean transforming a discussion from territorial disputes and historical grievances to shared goals like peace, stability, and prosperity for both nations.

The Power Of Positive Language

One of the first steps in reframing is the conscious use of positive language. Instead of focusing on accusations and blame, mediators encourage parties to express their needs and desires constructively. For instance, statements like "They're violating our sovereignty" could be reframed to "We seek recognition and respect for our national boundaries." This subtle shift in language can significantly reduce defensiveness, fostering an environment where mutual understanding can flourish.

Finding Common Ground

Central to the process of reframing is the identification of common interests and goals. Despite the deep-seated tensions between Ukraine and Russia, both nations share a desire for the well-being of their people, economic stability, and regional security. By highlighting these shared objectives, mediation can shift the focus from what divides the parties to what unites them, laying the groundwork for cooperative solutions.

Generating New Perspectives

Drawing on the insights of psychologist Alice Miller, we recognize that past traumas, whether personal or collective, can profoundly influence present conflicts. Reframing in mediation involves helping parties to see beyond their historical narratives of victimhood or aggression, encouraging them to envision a future defined by mutual respect and collaboration. This perspective shift is crucial in breaking the cycle of resentment and retaliation that often characterizes the Ukraine-Russia conflict.

Encouraging Empathy And Understanding

Reframing also plays a vital role in fostering empathy. By encouraging each party to view the conflict from the other's perspective, mediators can cultivate a deeper understanding of the fears, needs, and motivations driving the opposing side. This empathetic approach can dismantle stereotypes and mistrust, making it easier for parties to engage in meaningful dialogue and negotiation.

Navigating Power Imbalances

In international conflicts like that between Ukraine and Russia, power imbalances can significantly complicate mediation efforts. Reframing helps to address these disparities by ensuring that the voices and concerns of all parties are heard and valued equally. This approach not only promotes fairness but also enhances the legitimacy and acceptability of the mediation process and its outcomes.

Creating A Vision For The Future

Ultimately, reframing in mediation is about helping parties to envision a shared, positive future. For Ukraine and Russia, this could mean imagining a region where borders are respected, cultural differences are celebrated, and economic collaboration leads to prosperity for all. By focusing on this vision, mediation can inspire both nations to take concrete steps towards peace and reconciliation.

Reframing For Peace, Cooperation, Respect

In the face of the ongoing conflict between Ukraine and Russia, the technique of reframing offers a ray of hope. By shifting perspectives, language, and focus, mediation can pave the way for peace, understanding, and mutual prosperity.

By leveraging the power of reframing we can help both nations and individuals transcend their differences and build a future marked by cooperation and respect. The journey may be long and fraught with challenges, but with patience, empathy, and a commitment to positive change, a peaceful resolution is within reach.

3. More Than 700 Idioms And Phrases Reframed For Life And Peace

Here's my collection of more than 700 idioms and phrases, along with suggestions on how to see them in a new light, turning shadows into brightness, reframing darkness into light.

Feel free to come up with your own interpretations and join in making the world a brighter, more hopeful place for everyone.

1. "A good death" becomes "A meaningful life." Shifting the focus to the significance of one's life journey fosters a sense of purpose and the pursuit of impactful, positive legacies.

2. "A warrior's death" becomes "A warrior's resolve for peace." This reframing honors the strength and determination of a warrior but redirects these qualities towards achieving and maintaining peace.

3. "Adversaries in conflict" becomes "Partners in peace." This reframing shifts the focus from opposition to collaboration, emphasizing the potential for both nations to work together towards a common goal of peace, highlighting the mutual benefits of cooperation over conflict.

4. "Against all odds" becomes "Fueled by faith." It shifts the focus from the daunting nature of challenges to the strength derived from belief in oneself and the cause, emphasizing the

power of positive conviction.

5. "<u>Against all odds</u>" becomes "<u>With all possibilities.</u>" This reframing shifts the focus from the challenges that seem insurmountable to the potential opportunities that lie within every situation, emphasizing an optimistic outlook on overcoming adversity.

6. "<u>Amidst the ashes</u>" becomes "<u>Within the seedbed.</u>" This reframing suggests that even in the wake of destruction, there is fertile ground for new life and opportunities, emphasizing the potential for rebirth and growth that can follow after loss.

7. "<u>Amidst the ruins</u>" becomes "<u>Amidst the foundations.</u>" This reframing suggests that what may appear as destruction also serves as the groundwork for new structures, emphasizing the potential for rebuilding and starting anew.

8. "<u>Amidst the ruins</u>" becomes "<u>Amidst the seeds of renewal.</u>" This reframing suggests that even in the aftermath of destruction, there is the potential for new beginnings and growth, much like seeds sprouting in the ruins of old structures.

9. "<u>An eye for an eye</u>" becomes "<u>A hand in friendship.</u>" This reframing moves from the idea of retribution to one of extending goodwill and reconciliation, emphasizing the power of forgiveness and unity.

10. "<u>Arm for battle</u>" becomes "<u>Equip for peace.</u>" The focus here is on preparing oneself with the tools and mindset necessary for fostering peace, rather than gearing up for warfare.

11. "<u>Armies of foes</u>" becomes "<u>Legions of peacemakers.</u>" This reframing suggests that those once seen as enemies can become the strongest advocates for peace, highlighting the transformative potential of changing roles from combatants to champions of harmony.

12. "<u>Armies of opponents</u>" becomes "<u>Teams of collaborators.</u>" Instead of viewing others as adversaries, this phrase suggests

seeing potential partners in creating solutions, highlighting cooperation over competition.

13. "Armistice of the defeated" becomes "Alliance of the determined." This reframing turns a cessation of hostilities due to defeat into a proactive union of those committed to a common cause, emphasizing determination and collective strength.

14. "Armored against the world" becomes "Open to understanding." This reframing suggests moving from a defensive stance to a posture of openness and curiosity about the world, emphasizing the value of empathy and connection over isolation.

15. "Ashes of destruction" becomes "Soil of renewal." It transforms the residue of devastation into fertile ground for new beginnings, highlighting the regenerative potential that follows the clearing away of the old.

16. "Assault on the senses" becomes "Awakening to new sensations." This reframing suggests a shift from being overwhelmed to becoming acutely aware of and receptive to new experiences, emphasizing growth through new sensory experiences.

17. "Avalanche of despair" becomes "Snowfall of hope." This reframing changes the narrative from an overwhelming force of hopelessness to gentle flakes of optimism, promoting the idea that hope accumulates and covers the landscape with potential for renewal.

18. "Avalanche of problems" becomes "Stepping stones of solutions." Instead of an overwhelming force of issues, this phrase envisions manageable segments that lead to resolution, highlighting the potential to navigate through challenges systematically.

19. "Barrage of criticism" becomes "Rainfall of feedback." This reframing suggests transforming harsh criticism into

constructive feedback, seen as nourishing like rain, promoting growth and improvement rather than causing damage.

20. "Barricades of division" becomes "Bridges of unity." This reframing suggests transforming obstacles that separate people into structures that bring them together, emphasizing the importance of overcoming divisions to foster unity.

21. "Barricades of doubt" becomes "Bridges of confidence." Instead of obstacles created by uncertainty, this phrase envisions pathways built on self-assurance and trust, promoting the idea that confidence can connect us to our goals and aspirations.

22. "Barricades of fear" becomes "Bulwarks of bravery." Instead of obstacles created by fear, this phrase envisions protective structures that are fortified by acts of courage, promoting the idea that bravery can shield and support us.

23. "Barricades to understanding" becomes "Gateways to empathy." This reframing suggests that what once obstructed comprehension can become the entry point for deep emotional connection, emphasizing the transformative power of empathy.

24. "Barriers to peace" becomes "Bridges to understanding." Instead of focusing on what obstructs harmony, this phrase highlights the construction of connections that foster comprehension and empathy, promoting the idea that overcoming obstacles begins with seeking to understand each other.

25. "Battered by experiences" becomes "Enriched by experiences." This reframing suggests that life's challenges don't just wear us down; they also add depth and richness to our character, providing valuable lessons that contribute to our personal narrative.

26. "Battered by life's storms" becomes "Shaped by life's lessons." This reframing suggests that rather than being worn down by challenges, individuals are educated and molded

by them, emphasizing the personal growth that comes from overcoming adversity.

27. "Battered by the storm" becomes "Cleansed by the rain." This reframing suggests that the challenges we face can also wash away the old, making way for fresh starts and new growth, emphasizing the rejuvenating aspect of difficult experiences.

28. "Battered by the storm" becomes "Strengthened by the challenge." This reframing suggests that the trials we face can serve to fortify our resolve and character, much like a tree's roots grow stronger in response to the wind's resistance.

29. "Battle scars" becomes "Badges of resilience." This reframing moves from marks of injury to symbols of endurance and strength, promoting the recognition of resilience as a virtue honed through overcoming challenges.

30. "Battle till death" becomes "Strive for harmony." This phrase promotes the pursuit of balance and agreement, suggesting that efforts should be directed towards peaceful coexistence rather than conflict.

31. "Battleground of wills" becomes "Symphony of collaboration." Instead of a place where wills clash, this phrase envisions a harmonious blend of efforts, where different strengths come together to create something greater than the sum of its parts.

32. "Battlegrounds" becomes "Grounds for dialogue." Instead of areas marked by strife, this reframing envisions spaces where open conversations can occur, promoting the idea that communication is key to resolving differences and fostering peace.

33. "Battlegrounds" becomes "Meeting grounds." This reframing moves from places of conflict to spaces where people come together to share and learn, promoting the idea of commonality and shared human experience.

34. "Battlegrounds" becomes "Meeting grounds." Instead of areas marked by warfare, this phrase envisions spaces where dialogue and understanding can flourish, promoting the idea that shared spaces can be venues for reconciliation and mutual respect.

35. "Battles for dominance" becomes "Collaborations for mutual success." Instead of competing to be the top, this phrase suggests working together to achieve shared goals, emphasizing the benefits of cooperative efforts over confrontational tactics.

36. "Battles lost" becomes "Lessons learned." This reframing shifts the focus from defeat to the valuable insights gained from each experience, emphasizing that every setback is an opportunity for growth and improvement.

37. "Battles of attrition" becomes "Endurances of spirit." This reframing shifts from a focus on wearing down the opposition through prolonged conflict to highlighting the resilience and perseverance of the human spirit, emphasizing the strength found in enduring challenges.

38. "Battles of wills" becomes "Confluences of ideas." Instead of clashing egos, this phrase envisions the merging of diverse thoughts and perspectives, promoting the idea that from the meeting of minds can come innovative solutions.

39. "Battle-scarred" becomes "Experience-embellished." Instead of viewing scars as mere reminders of conflict, this phrase suggests they are marks of wisdom and growth, highlighting the valuable lessons learned through trials.

40. "Battle-scarred" becomes "Experience-emboldened." It changes the narrative from marks of conflict to symbols of the wisdom and strength gained through challenges, highlighting how experiences, even difficult ones, contribute to personal growth and fortitude.

41. "Battle-worn" becomes "Experience-rich." This reframing

shifts the focus from the weariness of conflict to the wealth of experience gained, emphasizing the value and wisdom that come from facing and overcoming challenges.

42. "<u>Battling against the odds</u>" becomes "<u>Embracing the journey of hope.</u>" This reframing suggests a shift from struggle to an optimistic embrace of life's challenges, highlighting the courage to pursue hopeful outcomes despite difficulties.

43. "<u>Battling the storm</u>" becomes "<u>Embracing the winds of change.</u>" This reframing suggests using the challenges faced during turbulent times as a means to drive positive change, emphasizing adaptability and the transformative power of adversity.

44. "<u>Bearing arms</u>" becomes "<u>Extending olive branches.</u>" This reframing suggests moving from the readiness for combat to offering symbols of peace and reconciliation, emphasizing the importance of gestures that promote understanding and harmony.

45. "<u>Bearing burdens</u>" becomes "<u>Gathering strength.</u>" Instead of highlighting the weight of challenges, this phrase suggests accumulating resilience and power through the experiences, promoting a narrative of growth through adversity.

46. "<u>Bearing the scars</u>" becomes "<u>Embracing the marks of resilience.</u>" This reframing shifts the focus from the pain and damage to the strength and endurance they represent, highlighting how overcoming challenges can shape us positively.

47. "<u>Besieged by despair</u>" becomes "<u>Surrounded by support.</u>" This reframing suggests that even when feeling overwhelmed by negative emotions, one is encircled by a community ready to offer help and encouragement, emphasizing the availability of support.

48. "<u>Bite the bullet</u>" becomes "<u>Savor the moment.</u>" This reframing suggests embracing and enjoying life's experiences rather than enduring pain or difficulty with resignation,

promoting an attitude of appreciation and presence.

49. "<u>Blaze of gunfire</u>" becomes "<u>Beacon of dialogue.</u>" This reframing shifts from the imagery of combat to the light of conversation, emphasizing the potential for communication to illuminate paths to understanding and resolution.

50. "<u>Bleak outcomes</u>" becomes "<u>Opportunities for growth.</u>" This reframing shifts the focus from negative results to the potential for learning and development, emphasizing that every challenge presents a chance to grow stronger and wiser.

51. "<u>Blind alleys of conflict</u>" becomes "<u>Open roads of dialogue.</u>" This reframing suggests moving from seemingly dead-end situations in disputes to pathways that encourage conversation and understanding, emphasizing the potential for resolution through open communication.

52. "<u>Blinded by vengeance</u>" becomes "<u>Enlightened by forgiveness.</u>" This reframing suggests moving from a desire for retribution to gaining insight and peace through the act of forgiveness, emphasizing the clarity and liberation it brings.

53. "<u>Blitz of aggression</u>" becomes "<u>Breeze of assertiveness.</u>" This reframing suggests a shift from an overwhelming force to a gentle yet firm presence, emphasizing the importance of standing up for oneself in a calm and collected manner.

54. "<u>Blizzard of confusion</u>" becomes "<u>Clarity of purpose.</u>" This reframing shifts from a state of bewilderment to a focused sense of direction, promoting the idea that navigating through confusion can lead to a stronger understanding of one's goals.

55. "<u>Blood, sweat, and tears</u>" becomes "<u>Heart, soul, and smiles.</u>" The focus here is on investing one's full emotional and spiritual energy into creating joy and satisfaction, rather than enduring hardship.

56. "<u>Bound by past mistakes</u>" becomes "<u>Informed by past lessons.</u>" This reframing shifts the focus from being trapped

by previous errors to being educated and guided by them, emphasizing growth and the acquisition of wisdom through experience.

57. "Brace for impact" becomes "Prepare for renewal." This reframing suggests readiness not for collision but for rejuvenation and new beginnings, encouraging a mindset geared towards recovery and growth.

58. "Bracing for a loss" becomes "Preparing for a lesson." This reframing suggests that instead of anticipating defeat, one is getting ready to learn something valuable, emphasizing growth and the acquisition of knowledge from every situation.

59. "Breaking down" becomes "Building up." This reframing transforms a moment of collapse into an opportunity for construction and development, highlighting the potential for renewal and growth.

60. "Breaking enemy lines" becomes "Building bridges of understanding." This reframing suggests moving from aggressive tactics to fostering connections and empathy, emphasizing the importance of mutual understanding in resolving conflicts.

61. "Breaking point" becomes "Turning point." This reframing suggests that moments of extreme stress or difficulty can also serve as pivotal moments for change, emphasizing opportunities for transformation and growth rather than collapse.

62. "Breaking under pressure" becomes "Shaping under guidance." Instead of succumbing to stress, this phrase suggests being molded and improved by experiences, emphasizing growth through adversity with the right support and mindset.

63. "Bullet-riddled past" becomes "Tapestry of survival." Instead of focusing on the damage and violence, this phrase highlights the intricate and resilient story of survival, weaving together experiences into a narrative of strength.

64. "Bullets of hate" becomes "Words of kindness." It shifts

from the imagery of violence to the power of compassionate communication, promoting the idea that kind words can heal and build bridges where hostility once prevailed.

65. "Bunker down" becomes "Rise up." Instead of preparing for isolation or defense, this phrase encourages standing tall and facing challenges head-on, promoting action and courage.

66. "Bunker mentality" becomes "Open-door policy." Instead of a defensive and isolated stance, this phrase suggests a welcoming and inclusive approach, fostering communication and collaboration.

67. "Burning bridges" becomes "Building bridges." It changes the act of destroying relationships into creating connections, emphasizing reconciliation and the strengthening of bonds.

68. "Burning bridges" becomes "Building new pathways." This reframing suggests moving from destroying connections to creating new opportunities for relationships and understanding, emphasizing constructive action over severance.

69. "Burning bridges" becomes "Lighting the way." Instead of focusing on the destruction of relationships or opportunities, this phrase suggests using past experiences to illuminate the path forward, promoting learning and growth.

70. "Calm before the storm" becomes "Peace before the promise." This reframing suggests that tranquility precedes not a destructive event but the hopeful anticipation of positive developments.

71. "Cannot continue to live unless ..." becomes "We choose to live by ..."

72. "Carnage of war" becomes "Canvas of peace." It transforms the image of destruction into a blank slate for creating a peaceful future, highlighting the potential for rebuilding and harmony.

73. "Casualties of battle" becomes "Catalysts for change." This

reframing moves from the losses incurred during conflict to the motivation they provide for societal transformation, emphasizing the drive for improvement that can arise from tragedy.

74. "Casualties of circumstance" becomes "Graduates of resilience." It shifts the focus from being victims of external factors to being individuals who have learned and emerged stronger, highlighting the capacity to adapt and thrive.

75. "Casualties of circumstance" becomes "Victors of versatility." It shifts the focus from being victims of uncontrollable events to champions who adapt and thrive, emphasizing the human ability to navigate and succeed despite unpredictable conditions.

76. "Casualties of the battlefield" becomes "Champions of resilience." Instead of focusing on the losses of conflict, this phrase highlights the enduring spirit of those who face adversity, recognizing their courage and the inspiration they provide.

77. "Casualties of war" becomes "Beacons of resilience." Instead of focusing on the losses, this phrase highlights the strength and endurance of those affected by conflict, promoting the idea that adversity can lead to remarkable demonstrations of human resilience.

78. "Casualties of war" becomes "Catalysts for peace." It shifts the narrative from the losses of conflict to the driving forces for creating peace, suggesting that the desire to prevent further loss can motivate peacebuilding efforts.

79. "Casualties of war" becomes "Catalysts for unity." This reframing suggests that the losses experienced can serve as a powerful motivation for coming together, emphasizing how shared grief can lead to a stronger, united front against further violence and division.

80. "Casualties of war" becomes "Harbingers of change." Instead of focusing on the losses, this phrase suggests that

such profound events can catalyze significant transformations, promoting the idea that from great sacrifice can come substantial progress.

81. "Casualties of war" becomes "Heroes of resilience." Instead of highlighting loss, this phrase celebrates the strength and perseverance of those affected by conflict, recognizing their courage and the inspiration they provide.

82. "Casualty count" becomes "Survivor's tally." Instead of focusing on the numbers of those lost, this phrase highlights those who have persevered, emphasizing the human capacity to endure and the importance of honoring survival.

83. "Casualty of war" becomes "Beacon of hope." Instead of a term that signifies loss and suffering, this phrase suggests that individuals affected by conflict can become symbols of resilience and the human spirit's capacity to overcome adversity.

84. "Casualty of war" becomes "Catalyst for change." This reframing turns a term for loss into a term for transformation, suggesting that every setback in conflict can be a driving force for improvement and evolution.

85. "Caught in a crossfire" becomes "Nurtured in a crossroads." It transforms the imagery from being trapped in conflict to being at a place of decision and growth, emphasizing the opportunities for choice and change that arise from difficult situations.

86. "Caught in a deadlock" becomes "Engaged in a dialogue." This reframing moves from a standstill in conflict to active participation in conversation, emphasizing the potential for progress through open communication and mutual understanding.

87. "Caught in a storm" becomes "Nurtured by the rain." Moving from a narrative of being trapped and battered by difficulties to one of receiving sustenance and growth from challenges, this reframing promotes the idea that hardships can

lead to renewal and flourishing.

88. "Caught in a web" becomes "Weaving a tapestry." This reframing moves from a sense of entrapment to the active creation of something beautiful and interconnected, highlighting the potential for crafting a rich and meaningful narrative from life's complexities.

89. "Caught in the crossfire" becomes "Bridging the divide." Instead of being trapped in conflict, this phrase emphasizes the active role in connecting opposing sides, fostering a sense of agency in peacebuilding.

90. "Caught in the crossfire" becomes "Embraced in the crossroads." It shifts from being an unintended target to being at a place of decision and opportunity, emphasizing the potential for making pivotal choices that lead to positive outcomes.

91. "Caught in the crosshairs" becomes "Centered in the heart of change." Moving from being a target to being at the core of transformation, this reframing emphasizes an active role in shaping and directing positive change.

92. "Caught in the fray" becomes "Engaged in the solution." It shifts the focus from being entangled in conflict to actively participating in finding resolutions, emphasizing proactive involvement and problem-solving.

93. "Chains of conflict" becomes "Links of partnership." It transforms the imagery from bondage to connection, promoting the idea that strong relationships can be forged in the aftermath of strife, leading to robust partnerships based on mutual goals.

94. "Chains of oppression" becomes "Links of liberation." It shifts from the imagery of bondage to the concept of connection that frees, highlighting the strength found in solidarity and the collective fight for freedom.

95. "Chains of resentment" becomes "Ribbons of forgiveness." Instead of bonds that tie one to past hurts, this phrase suggests

delicate strands that connect individuals through the act of pardoning, highlighting the freedom found in forgiveness.

96. "Charge into the fray" becomes "Advance towards unity." This reframing suggests moving forward not to engage in battle but to come together, emphasizing progress towards collective harmony rather than conflict.

97. "Clash of civilizations" becomes "Fusion of cultures." Instead of highlighting conflict between societies, this phrase suggests the blending and enriching interactions that can occur, promoting the beauty of cultural exchange and mutual enrichment.

98. "Clash of ideologies" becomes "Exchange of perspectives." Instead of highlighting the conflict between differing beliefs, this phrase suggests a mutual sharing of views, promoting understanding and respect for diverse opinions.

99. "Clash of interests" becomes "Convergence of ideas." It shifts the focus from conflicting interests to the point where different ideas meet, suggesting that from the diversity of thoughts, innovative solutions can emerge.

100. "Clash of titans" becomes "Meeting of minds." Instead of a confrontation between powerful forces, this phrase envisions a productive dialogue between influential thinkers, highlighting the potential for constructive outcomes from discussions.

101. "Clash of wills" becomes "Harmony of hearts." This reframing moves from a confrontation of desires to a unity of intentions, highlighting the potential for empathy and mutual understanding in resolving differences.

102. "Collateral damage" becomes "Collaborative gains." Shifting the focus from unintended harm to mutual benefits, this reframing highlights the positive outcomes that can arise from working together.

103. "Collateral damage" becomes "Collateral growth." It

shifts the focus from unintended negative consequences to the unexpected positive developments that can arise even in difficult situations.

104. "Collateral damage" becomes "Impetus for care." Instead of focusing on the unintended harm caused in conflicts, this phrase suggests using such outcomes as a motivation to increase efforts in protection and aid, emphasizing a commitment to minimizing harm and fostering care.

105. "Collateral damage" becomes "Seeds of renewal." It transforms the notion of unintended harm into the potential for new beginnings, highlighting how every adverse event can also be a starting point for growth and positive change.

106. "Collateral damage" becomes "Unintended growth." It shifts the focus from the unintended negative consequences of actions to the unexpected positive changes that can arise, highlighting the potential for learning and improvement even in difficult circumstances.

107. "Collateral damage" becomes "Unintended growth." Instead of focusing on the negative side effects of an action, this phrase highlights the unexpected positive developments, encouraging a search for silver linings even in difficult situations.

108. "Combat fatigue" becomes "Renewal of spirit." Instead of a state of exhaustion from conflict, this phrase suggests a period of rejuvenation and revitalization, highlighting the potential for rest and recovery to restore one's energy and purpose.

109. "Combat zone" becomes "Dialogue arena." Instead of a place for fighting, this phrase envisions an area where open, honest conversations occur, emphasizing the potential for resolving conflicts through communication.

110. "Combat zone" becomes "Recovery zone." It shifts the focus from an area of active fighting to one of healing and rebuilding, highlighting the potential for areas once marred by conflict to

transform into spaces of renewal.

111. "Conflict-ridden" becomes "Cooperation-driven." This reframing moves from a state of ongoing discord to a commitment to working together, promoting the pursuit of mutual goals and shared success.

112. "Confronting the enemy" becomes "Engaging with a challenger." This phrase changes the adversarial tone to one of competition and challenge, where the 'enemy' is seen as a worthy opponent from whom one can learn and grow.

113. "Conquer the enemy" becomes "Embrace the ally." This reframing suggests moving from defeating opponents to welcoming partners, promoting peace and cooperation over victory in conflict.

114. "Conquering fears" becomes "Embracing courage." This phrase suggests not just overcoming fears but actively adopting a courageous approach to life's challenges, highlighting the empowerment that comes with facing fears head-on.

115. "Consigned to the earth" becomes "Sown into the fabric of life." This reframing suggests that in death, we are not merely buried but are sown like seeds into the ongoing cycle of life, contributing to the growth and renewal of the world.

116. "Corridors of power" becomes "Pathways of empowerment." It shifts from the notion of exclusive control to the democratization of influence, highlighting opportunities for all individuals to find their strength and agency.

117. "Courting death" becomes "Courting courage." This reframing suggests actively pursuing bravery and resilience, which can lead to overcoming obstacles without resorting to fatalistic measures.

118. "Craters of devastation" becomes "Wellsprings of renewal." Instead of focusing on the scars left by adversity, this phrase envisions sources of new beginnings and growth, highlighting

the resilience and regenerative power inherent in communities and individuals.

119. "Cries of despair" becomes "Echoes of resilience." Instead of focusing on the sounds of sorrow, this phrase highlights the enduring spirit and strength that emerge in response to adversity, promoting the idea that resilience grows louder in the face of challenges.

120. "Cries of pain" becomes "Voices of strength." Instead of focusing on expressions of suffering, this phrase suggests that vocalizing our struggles is an act of courage, emphasizing the power in sharing our stories of resilience.

121. "Cries of war" becomes "Calls for peace." It shifts the focus from the sounds of conflict to the voices advocating for harmony, emphasizing the desire and efforts for peaceful resolutions.

122. "Cries of war" becomes "Chants for peace." Shifting from the sounds of conflict to the collective voice calling for harmony, this phrase promotes the power of a united call for tranquility and coexistence.

123. "Crossfire of opinions" becomes "Confluence of perspectives." Instead of a chaotic exchange where ideas clash destructively, this phrase envisions a meeting place where diverse viewpoints can flow together to form a richer understanding.

124. "Crossing the Rubicon" becomes "Bridging the gap." This shifts from a point of no return to an effort to connect and reconcile, emphasizing efforts to overcome divisions and build understanding.

125. "Crushed by failure" becomes "Sculpted by feedback." Instead of viewing failure as a destructive force, this phrase suggests seeing it as constructive criticism that shapes and refines one's path, highlighting the value of learning from setbacks.

126. "Cutting losses" becomes "Cultivating gains." Instead of focusing on what has been given up, this phrase emphasizes

the growth and benefits that can be nurtured from difficult situations.

127. "Cutting through the enemy lines" becomes "Connecting across new horizons." This reframing suggests building bridges rather than severing ties, emphasizing the importance of reaching out and establishing new relationships for a collective future.

128. "Damaged by conflict" becomes "Sculpted by experiences." It transforms the narrative from being harmed to being shaped by life's trials, emphasizing that our experiences, including those involving conflict, contribute to our depth and complexity as individuals.

129. "Damaged goods" becomes "Recovered treasures." This reframing moves from the idea of irreparable loss to the value found in restoration and resilience, celebrating the worth of what has been healed or saved.

130. "Dancing with death" becomes "Dancing with life." This reframing shifts the focus from flirting with danger to celebrating life's vibrancy and movement, encouraging an engagement with the present moment and the joy it can bring.

131. "Deadlocked in battle" becomes "United in purpose." Moving from a stalemate in conflict to a shared commitment, this reframing emphasizes the power of common goals to bring people together, even from opposing sides.

132. "Deadly silence" becomes "Reflective quiet." It shifts the focus from a foreboding absence of sound to a peaceful space for contemplation, promoting the value of silence for thoughtful introspection and calm.

133. "Decimated ranks" becomes "Consolidated strengths." It shifts from the losses within a group to the combined power and capabilities of those who remain, emphasizing the potential for a smaller but more unified team.

134. "Decimated ranks" becomes "Consolidated unity." This

reframing moves from the idea of reduced numbers to the concept of strengthened solidarity among those who remain, emphasizing the potential for a more unified group.

135. "Defending my turf" becomes "Sharing my space." Instead of a defensive stance, this reframing promotes inclusivity and the idea of coexisting and sharing resources or ideas with others.

136. "Defensive positions" becomes "Open stances." This reframing moves from a mindset prepared for attack to one that is welcoming and ready for engagement, promoting a posture of receptivity and dialogue.

137. "Demilitarized zone" becomes "Harmonized zone." This reframing moves from a space defined by the absence of military presence to one characterized by the active pursuit of balance and unity among former adversaries.

138. "Demilitarized zone" becomes "Zone of peace." Instead of an area simply free from military presence, this phrase envisions a space actively dedicated to tranquility and harmony, emphasizing the positive aspects of demilitarization.

139. "Demolished hopes" becomes "Blueprints for the future." Instead of focusing on what has been torn down, this reframing suggests laying out plans for what will be built next, emphasizing forward-thinking and constructive planning.

140. "Demolished hopes" becomes "Blueprints for the future." It shifts from the despair of shattered expectations to the constructive planning stage of what's to come, emphasizing the opportunity to rebuild dreams with a stronger foundation.

141. "Demoralized troops" becomes "Heartened team." This reframing moves from a sense of discouragement to one of encouragement and support, promoting the idea of lifting each other's spirits and strengthening collective resolve.

142. "Derailed by adversity" becomes "Redirected towards new opportunities." Moving from a narrative of interruption and loss

to one of discovery and chance, this reframing promotes the idea that challenges can lead to unforeseen and rewarding paths.

143. "Desert of desolation" becomes "Oasis of opportunity." It transforms the image of a barren, lifeless place into a fertile spot brimming with chances for growth and renewal, promoting the idea that even the most desolate situations can harbor potential for positive change.

144. "Desert of desolation" becomes "Oasis of serenity." This reframing moves from an image of barren emptiness to a tranquil haven, promoting the idea that solitude can be a peaceful retreat for reflection and rejuvenation.

145. "Desert of isolation" becomes "Oasis of connection." Instead of an expanse of loneliness, this phrase envisions a welcoming place of community and belonging, emphasizing the importance of finding and nurturing relationships.

146. "Deserts of indifference" becomes "Oases of care." It shifts from barren landscapes of apathy to fertile spots rich with attention and concern, highlighting the potential for areas of warmth and support to emerge in even the most uncaring environments.

147. "Desolation of war" becomes "Seeds of peace." It transforms the imagery of war's destruction into the beginning of peace-making efforts, highlighting the potential for reconciliation and harmony to emerge from conflict.

148. "Destruction's aftermath" becomes "Reconstruction's dawn." It shifts the focus from the ruins left by devastation to the first light of rebuilding efforts, highlighting the opportunity to create something new and hopeful from the ashes.

149. "Destruction's path" becomes "Reconstruction's road." This reframing moves from the aftermath of devastation to the journey of rebuilding, promoting a focus on recovery and the positive actions taken towards restoration.

150. "Destruction's wake" becomes "Creation's cradle." Instead of focusing on what has been destroyed, this phrase suggests looking at what can now be created, emphasizing the potential for innovation and new beginnings.

151. "Die for honor" becomes "Live with honor." It suggests that honor is not only found in death but in the way one lives and conducts oneself, advocating for integrity and respect in all aspects of life.

152. "Dig in for a long war" becomes "Lay the foundation for lasting peace." Instead of preparing for prolonged conflict, this phrase encourages the establishment of a solid base for enduring harmony, focusing on the long-term benefits of peace-building efforts.

153. "Digging in one's heels" becomes "Planting seeds for compromise." This suggests moving from stubborn resistance to proactive efforts in finding middle ground, emphasizing the growth that comes from flexibility and understanding.

154. "Digging one's own grave" becomes "Planting seeds for the future." This shifts the narrative from self-destruction to nurturing potential, highlighting the actions we take today to cultivate a better tomorrow.

155. "Divided by borders" becomes "United by humanity." It shifts the focus from geographical and political divisions to the shared human experience, promoting the idea that common values and mutual human respect can bridge divides.

156. "Divided nations" becomes "United in humanity." It shifts the focus from political and territorial divisions to the shared human experience, highlighting the common ground that exists beyond borders and encouraging empathy and mutual respect.

157. "Divides of opinion" becomes "Unity in diversity." This reframing moves from highlighting differences that separate to celebrating the strength that comes from varied perspectives,

promoting the idea that diversity enriches and strengthens communal bonds.

158. "Divides of war" becomes "Bridges of dialogue." It shifts from the separations created by conflict to the potential for communication and understanding that can bridge those gaps, emphasizing reconciliation and unity.

159. "Do or die" becomes "Do and thrive." This encourages proactive engagement with challenges, highlighting the potential for growth and success in place of resignation to a fatalistic outcome.

160. "Down in the trenches" becomes "Rising to the occasion." Instead of being mired in difficult circumstances, this phrase encourages rising above challenges and demonstrating resilience and leadership.

161. "Draw battle lines" becomes "Sketch paths of peace." This reframing moves from creating divisions to drafting routes that lead to harmony, highlighting the importance of planning and designing for peaceful outcomes.

162. "Draw the sword" becomes "Extend the hand." Instead of preparing for combat, this phrase encourages reaching out for diplomacy and friendship, highlighting the power of connection over confrontation.

163. "Drawing the last breath" becomes "Breathing in new possibilities." Instead of marking an end, this phrase suggests inhaling the fresh air of new opportunities, symbolizing the continuous cycle of life and the potential for renewal.

164. "Drenched in sweat" becomes "Bathed in perseverance." This reframing moves from the discomfort of exertion to the cleansing experience of persisting through challenges, highlighting the refreshing and rewarding aspect of hard work.

165. "Drowning in despair" becomes "Swimming towards hope." It transforms the feeling of being overwhelmed by negative

emotions into an active pursuit of optimism and brighter prospects, emphasizing movement towards positivity.

166. "Drowning in problems" becomes "Swimming towards solutions." It transforms the feeling of being overwhelmed by issues into an active pursuit of resolutions, emphasizing agency and the journey towards improvement.

167. "Dust of destruction" becomes "Seeds of construction." It transforms the imagery of ruin into the potential for building anew, promoting the idea that from the remnants of the old, new structures and relationships can be forged.

168. "Dying for a cause" becomes "Living for a purpose." This reframing moves from sacrifice to active engagement, emphasizing the importance of dedicating one's life to meaningful goals and the impact of positive action.

169. "Echoes of aggression" becomes "Melodies of accord." It changes the narrative from the remnants of hostility to the harmonious sounds of agreement and cooperation, emphasizing the shift from conflict to collaboration.

170. "Echoes of aggression" becomes "Whispers of compromise." Instead of reverberating with the sounds of conflict, this phrase suggests the quiet but powerful presence of willingness to find middle ground, highlighting the importance of soft diplomacy and the strength found in flexibility.

171. "Echoes of agony" becomes "Resonance of recovery." This reframing moves from the reverberations of pain to the sound of healing and progress, promoting the idea that recovery can be a powerful and uplifting process.

172. "Echoes of agony" becomes "Voices of healing." It transforms the remnants of pain into the sound of recovery, highlighting the collective and individual journeys towards healing and the strength found in shared experiences.

173. "Echoes of battle" becomes "Harmonies of peace." Instead

of the lingering sounds of conflict, this phrase envisions the resonant tones of harmony and tranquility, emphasizing the shift towards peaceful coexistence.

174. "Echoes of conflict" becomes "Whispers of harmony." This reframing suggests moving from the reverberations of past disputes to the subtle, growing sounds of agreement and peace, emphasizing the quiet yet powerful shift towards unity.

175. "Echoes of despair" becomes "Melodies of hope." Instead of reverberations of hopelessness, this phrase suggests the presence of uplifting tunes that inspire optimism, highlighting the transition from despair to a hopeful outlook.

176. "Echoes of discord" becomes "Harmonies of accord." This reframing suggests moving from the residual noise of disagreement to the creation of a unified and pleasant sound, emphasizing the potential for disparate voices to come together in agreement and create something beautiful.

177. "Echoes of gunfire" becomes "Echoes of unity." This reframing shifts from the sound of conflict to the sound of people coming together, emphasizing the potential for collective action and solidarity in the aftermath of strife.

178. "Echoes of gunfire" becomes "Whispers of dialogue." Instead of the reverberations of conflict, this phrase highlights the quiet yet powerful conversations that pave the way for peace, underscoring the strength found in calm communication.

179. "Echoes of loss" becomes "Melodies of memory." This reframing transforms the focus from what has been lost to the cherished memories that remain, emphasizing the enduring connection and the beauty found in recollection.

180. "Echoes of loss" becomes "Resonances of legacy." Instead of focusing on what has been taken away, this phrase suggests the enduring impact and influence of what has been left behind, promoting the idea of lasting contributions.

181. "Echoes of loss" becomes "Voices of gain." This reframing shifts from dwelling on what has been taken away to celebrating what has been learned or acquired, emphasizing the positive aspects and growth that come from experiencing loss.

182. "Echoes of sorrow" becomes "Voices of resilience." Instead of focusing on the remnants of pain, this phrase highlights the strength and perseverance that emerge from adversity, celebrating the human capacity to recover and thrive.

183. "Echoes of violence" becomes "Whispers of peace." This reframing shifts from the remnants of conflict to the subtle, yet powerful, beginnings of peace, emphasizing the potential for quiet transformations towards harmony.

184. "Echoes of war" becomes "Whispers of reconciliation." This phrase suggests that amidst the noise of conflict, there are quiet, yet powerful, efforts towards understanding and coming together, emphasizing the potential for healing and unity even in challenging times.

185. "Eclipsed by tragedy" becomes "Illuminated by empathy." Moving from being overshadowed by misfortune to being lit by shared understanding and compassion, this phrase promotes the idea that empathy brings light to even the darkest situations.

186. "Edge of the abyss" becomes "Threshold of new horizons." Instead of depicting a precipice leading to darkness, this phrase suggests standing on the brink of discovery and opportunity, emphasizing forward momentum and exploration.

187. "Embrace martyrdom" becomes "Embrace hope." Encouraging hope over resignation to fate, this phrase supports a forward-looking perspective that anticipates positive outcomes and solutions.

188. "En garde" becomes "Open arms." Instead of preparing for a duel, this phrase invites a posture of welcome and acceptance, suggesting readiness for friendship and collaboration.

189. "End of the journey" becomes "Summit of experiences." Rather than seeing the conclusion of life as an end, this phrase frames it as reaching the pinnacle of one's life journey, filled with rich experiences and wisdom to be celebrated and shared.

190. "Endless warfare" becomes "Endless pursuit of peace." It shifts the focus from perpetual conflict to the continuous and determined effort to achieve peace, highlighting the relentless nature of the human spirit in seeking harmony.

191. "Enduring hardship" becomes "Embracing transformation." This reframing moves from passively suffering through tough times to actively accepting and using these experiences as catalysts for personal change and growth.

192. "Enemies at the gates" becomes "Future allies in waiting." Instead of viewing others as adversaries, this phrase suggests the possibility of transforming opposition into partnership, highlighting the potential for reconciliation and collaboration.

193. "Enemies of progress" becomes "Teachers of resilience." This reframing moves from viewing opposition as a barrier to seeing it as an opportunity to strengthen resolve and adaptability, emphasizing the lessons learned from facing resistance.

194. "Enemy combatants" becomes "Future partners for peace." It transforms the view of adversaries in conflict into potential collaborators in building peace, promoting the idea that today's opponents can become tomorrow's allies in creating a harmonious future.

195. "Enemy lines" becomes "Lines of communication." Instead of demarcating divisions and opposition, this phrase suggests opportunities for dialogue and understanding, promoting the idea that former barriers can become connections.

196. "Enemy lines" becomes "Lines of connection." Instead of demarcating separation and opposition, this phrase suggests opportunities for establishing relationships and understanding,

emphasizing bridges over barriers.

197. "Enemy lines" becomes "Lines of potential friendship." This reframing moves from viewing others as adversaries to seeing them as future friends, emphasizing the possibility of transforming relationships through understanding and empathy.

198. "Engulfed by grief" becomes "Embraced by healing." It changes the imagery from being overwhelmed by sorrow to being surrounded by the process of recovery, emphasizing the journey towards emotional restoration and peace.

199. "Engulfed in flames" becomes "Bathed in light." It changes the narrative from being consumed by destructive forces to being surrounded by illuminating and guiding energy, promoting a sense of hope and guidance.

200. "Engulfed in flames" becomes "Illuminated by flames." Instead of being consumed by destructive forces, this phrase suggests being enlightened and guided by the experience, highlighting the clarity and insight that can come from trials.

201. "Engulfed in warfare" becomes "Immersed in peacemaking." It changes the narrative from being consumed by conflict to being deeply involved in the process of creating peace, highlighting the active role in fostering harmony.

202. "Enlist for battle" becomes "Enlist for betterment." This reframing moves from signing up to fight to joining a cause that aims to improve conditions, emphasizing the positive impact one can have through active participation.

203. "Enter the battlefield" becomes "Join the roundtable." This reframing suggests coming together in discussion and negotiation, rather than entering a space of combat, promoting dialogue over discord.

204. "Entrenched beliefs" becomes "Evolving convictions." It transforms the notion of rigidly held views into the concept of beliefs that are open to growth and change, emphasizing the

positive aspects of adaptability and learning.

205. "Entrenched enemy" becomes "Potential partner." It shifts the view from a fixed adversary to a possible ally, promoting the idea that understanding and common interests can turn opposition into cooperation.

206. "Entrenched in battle" becomes "Rooted in courage." This reframing moves from a position of being stuck in conflict to being firmly planted in bravery, highlighting the strength and valor that come from facing adversity.

207. "Entrenched positions" becomes "Nurtured perspectives." Instead of stubbornly held views, this phrase suggests carefully cultivated and evolving viewpoints, promoting openness to change and growth.

208. "Enveloped in darkness" becomes "Cradled in potential." This reframing suggests that being surrounded by uncertainty or difficulty is also being in a place ripe with possibilities, promoting the idea that from darkness can emerge new light and opportunities.

209. "Erosion of trust" becomes "Cultivation of confidence." Instead of the gradual wearing away of faith in others, this phrase suggests actively nurturing and growing trust, promoting the idea that confidence can be built and strengthened over time.

210. "Eternal rest" becomes "Endless exploration." This shifts the narrative from a permanent cessation to an ongoing journey of discovery, emphasizing the continuous nature of growth and learning beyond any single lifetime.

211. "Explosions of anger" becomes "Sparks of passion." It shifts from the destructive imagery of rage to the constructive potential of intense enthusiasm, highlighting how strong emotions can be channeled into positive and productive endeavors.

212. "Explosive situation" becomes "Catalytic moment." Instead of a scenario prone to violence, this phrase suggests an

opportunity that accelerates significant change, promoting the idea of transformational events.

213. "Face mortality" becomes "Embrace vitality." It promotes a focus on the energy and vibrancy of life, encouraging actions that contribute to health, well-being, and the zest for living.

214. "Facing an uphill battle" becomes "Ascending towards shared goals." This reframing transforms a difficult struggle into a collaborative effort to reach a common summit, highlighting the positive journey and the unity of purpose.

215. "Facing defeat" becomes "Learning resilience." Instead of focusing on failure, this phrase emphasizes the lessons and strength gained from setbacks, promoting a mindset of continuous learning and bouncing back.

216. "Facing the final curtain" becomes "Embracing life's encore." This reframing suggests that instead of viewing life's end as a finality, we see it as a chance to appreciate and reflect on the moments that made life extraordinary, much like the encore of a cherished performance.

217. "Facing the firing squad" becomes "Joining the assembly of progress." Rather than confronting an end, this phrase suggests coming together to contribute to forward movement and collective improvement.

218. "Facing the void" becomes "Exploring the unknown." This reframing shifts from confronting emptiness to venturing into uncharted territory with curiosity and courage, highlighting the potential for discovery and new beginnings.

219. "Fading away" becomes "Becoming part of everything." This reframing implies that in death, we don't simply fade into nothingness; instead, we become an integral part of the larger tapestry of life and the universe.

220. "Fading into oblivion" becomes "Emerging into presence." Instead of disappearing into nothingness, this phrase emphasizes

coming into awareness and engagement with the world, highlighting the importance of being active and present in one's life.

221. "Fallen soldiers" becomes "Guardians of peace." Instead of focusing solely on the loss, this phrase honors those who have served by envisioning them as protectors of peace, highlighting their ultimate contribution to securing tranquility for the future.

222. "Falling into the abyss" becomes "Ascending towards potential." Instead of a descent into darkness, this phrase suggests an upward journey towards realizing one's capabilities and possibilities, promoting a vision of growth and ascent.

223. "Fears of escalation" becomes "Hopes for de-escalation." This reframing moves from anxiety about worsening conditions to optimism for calming tensions, emphasizing proactive efforts towards peace and the belief in positive outcomes.

224. "Fields of battle" becomes "Fields of reconciliation." Instead of areas marked by conflict, this phrase envisions spaces where differences are resolved and common ground is found, promoting the idea of healing and coming together.

225. "Fields of battle" becomes "Gardens of reconciliation." It transforms the imagery of conflict-ridden areas into spaces where healing and mutual understanding can grow, emphasizing peace-building over warfare.

226. "Fields of battle" becomes "Meadows of collaboration." Transforming a place of conflict into a space for cooperative efforts, this reframing focuses on the potential for joint ventures to flourish in an atmosphere of partnership.

227. "Fields of conflict" becomes "Meadows of mediation." It transforms the battleground into a peaceful setting for resolution, promoting the idea that every area of dispute can become a place where differences are resolved through dialogue.

228. "Fight fire with fire" becomes "Illuminate darkness with

light." This reframing moves away from retaliation to the idea of overcoming adversity with positivity and understanding, emphasizing constructive conflict resolution.

229. "Fight for survival" becomes "Unite for prosperity." This reframing moves from individual struggle to communal effort, emphasizing the benefits of coming together to create a thriving environment for all.

230. "Fight the enemy" becomes "Understand the adversary." It changes the narrative from confrontation to comprehension, highlighting the importance of empathy and understanding in resolving conflicts.

231. "Fight the good fight" becomes "Champion the good cause." It reframes the concept of struggle into one of advocacy, suggesting active support for positive change rather than combative actions.

232. "Fight to the bitter end" becomes "Work towards a sweet beginning." This reframing shifts from a grim determination to a hopeful dedication to creating a positive and fresh start, emphasizing constructive action.

233. "Fight to the death" becomes "Strive for life." Instead of engaging in a struggle with a fatal outcome, this phrase encourages efforts that affirm and enhance life, promoting a dedication to living fully and meaningfully.

234. "Fighting a losing battle" becomes "Advancing towards future victories." This reframing suggests that current struggles are steps towards future successes, highlighting the importance of perseverance and long-term vision.

235. "Fighting a losing battle" becomes "Paving the path to peace." This reframing shifts from a focus on defeat to the constructive efforts made towards achieving peace, emphasizing the value of every step taken in the direction of reconciliation.

236. "Fighting against the current" becomes "Flowing with the

river." Moving from resistance to adaptation, this reframing emphasizes the wisdom in aligning with circumstances and finding the path of least resistance to move forward.

237. "<u>Fighting against the tide</u>" becomes "<u>Sailing with the wind.</u>" This reframing moves from struggling against overwhelming forces to harnessing them for forward momentum, promoting the idea of working with circumstances rather than against them.

238. "<u>Fighting back tears</u>" becomes "<u>Cultivating empathy.</u>" It changes the narrative from suppressing emotions to understanding and sharing feelings, emphasizing emotional intelligence and connection.

239. "<u>Fighting for breath</u>" becomes "<u>Breathing in life.</u>" This reframing moves from a struggle for survival to an appreciation of being alive, emphasizing the act of taking in each moment and the vitality it brings.

240. "<u>Fighting on the front lines</u>" becomes "<u>Building bridges on the front lines.</u>" It shifts from combat to construction, highlighting efforts to connect and reconcile even in the midst of conflict, promoting peacebuilding as an active process.

241. "<u>Fighting to the last man</u>" becomes "<u>Standing united for a new beginning.</u>" Unity and the prospect of a fresh start inspire hope and collective action, steering the narrative towards constructive change rather than ultimate sacrifice.

242. "<u>Fighting tooth and nail</u>" becomes "<u>Working hand in hand.</u>" It shifts from a narrative of fierce combat to one of cooperation and mutual assistance, emphasizing the strength that comes from working together.

243. "<u>Fires of anger</u>" becomes "<u>Warmth of compassion.</u>" Instead of destructive flames fueled by rage, this phrase envisions a comforting heat that fosters care and kindness, promoting the healing nature of compassion.

244. "<u>Fires of vengeance</u>" becomes "<u>Lights of forgiveness.</u>"

This reframing suggests moving from the destructive blaze of retribution to the guiding light of pardon, promoting forgiveness as a path to peace and understanding.

245. "Firing at will" becomes "Aiming for accord." This reframing suggests a transition from indiscriminate conflict to targeted efforts for agreement, highlighting the importance of intentional actions toward peace.

246. "Firing lines" becomes "Lines of communication." It changes the imagery from preparation for combat to establishing open dialogues, emphasizing the power of words and negotiation in resolving conflicts.

247. "Firing lines" becomes "Lines of dialogue." It shifts the imagery from combat readiness to open channels of communication, promoting the idea that words and understanding are more powerful and effective than weapons.

248. "Firing squad" becomes "Firing up squad." It changes the narrative from a group executing punishment to a team inspiring and motivating each other, highlighting encouragement and support.

249. "Firing upon" becomes "Reaching out to." This reframing moves from an act of hostility to one of communication and connection, emphasizing the power of extending a hand in an effort to bridge gaps.

250. "Fog of conflict" becomes "Light of clarity." It shifts from confusion and uncertainty brought by strife to the illumination that comes with clear, peaceful intentions and actions, emphasizing the power of transparency and honesty in paving the way for peace.

251. "Fog of confusion" becomes "Clarity of insight." Instead of a lack of understanding, this phrase suggests the emergence of clear and valuable realizations, emphasizing the moments of enlightenment that can come from navigating uncertainty.

252. "Fog of despair" becomes "Clarity of hope." Instead of a dense, confusing mist of sorrow, this phrase envisions a clear, bright vision of optimism, emphasizing the emergence from darkness into a hopeful future.

253. "Fog of despair" becomes "Clarity of purpose." This reframing changes the narrative from being lost in hopelessness to finding a clear and meaningful direction, highlighting the motivational power of having a defined goal.

254. "Fog of despair" becomes "Light of resolve." It changes the narrative from being lost in hopelessness to finding direction through determination, highlighting the clarity and strength that come from decisive action.

255. "Fog of uncertainty" becomes "Clarity of conviction." It shifts from confusion and doubt to clear, strong beliefs, promoting the idea that certainty can emerge from the most unclear situations through introspection and determination.

256. "Fog of uncertainty" becomes "Mist of possibility." Instead of a dense fog that obscures vision and direction, this phrase suggests a lighter mist that hints at the myriad paths available, promoting optimism in the face of the unknown.

257. "Fog of war" becomes "Clarity of purpose." Instead of confusion and chaos, this phrase envisions a sharpened sense of mission and values that often crystallizes in challenging times, highlighting the focus and determination that adversity can inspire.

258. "Fog of war" becomes "Clarity of purpose." It changes the confusion and uncertainty of conflict to a clear and focused intention, highlighting the importance of maintaining a sense of direction amidst chaos.

259. "Fog of war" becomes "Light of understanding." This reframing transforms the confusion and lack of clarity associated with conflict into the illumination that comes from

seeking comprehension and insight, emphasizing the pursuit of knowledge and empathy.

260. "Fog of war" becomes "Sunrise of peace." Instead of a clouded, uncertain situation brought by conflict, this phrase suggests the dawning of a new era characterized by harmony and understanding, promoting the clarity and warmth that peace brings.

261. "Fortifying defenses" becomes "Opening hearts and minds." Moving away from a stance of protectionism to one of openness, this phrase encourages embracing new ideas and perspectives, fostering an environment of inclusivity and acceptance.

262. "Fortresses of solitude" becomes "Havens of community." It transforms the image of isolation into one of connection and support, highlighting the importance of communal spaces for recovery and unity.

263. "Frayed at the edges" becomes "Woven with care." It changes the narrative from coming apart to being carefully crafted, emphasizing the meticulous attention and intention that goes into creating a life of resilience and interconnectedness.

264. "Frayed by battle" becomes "Fortified by experience." This reframing suggests that the wear of conflict serves to strengthen character, promoting the idea that experiences, even harsh ones, contribute to personal fortitude.

265. "Frayed edges" becomes "Interwoven strengths." Instead of highlighting wear and tear, this phrase suggests the strength found in bringing together diverse elements, emphasizing unity and collective resilience.

266. "Frayed nerves" becomes "Strengthened resolve." Instead of highlighting the weariness of stress, this phrase suggests that such experiences can fortify one's determination, promoting the idea that overcoming tension builds character.

267. "Fraying at the edges" becomes "Weaving a stronger fabric." It changes the narrative from coming apart to creating something more robust and interconnected, emphasizing the strength that comes from unity and shared effort.

268. "Fraying at the seams" becomes "Stitching stronger ties." It changes the narrative from relationships coming apart to the careful work of mending and reinforcing them, emphasizing the importance of repairing and strengthening bonds.

269. "Friendly fire" becomes "Friendly support." Instead of an accidental harm among allies, this phrase emphasizes the intentional aid and backing provided by comrades, promoting the positive aspects of camaraderie and assistance.

270. "Front lines of battle" becomes "Frontiers of understanding." This reframing suggests that the most intense areas of conflict can become the leading edges of mutual comprehension and empathy, promoting the idea of progress through adversity.

271. "Front lines of war" becomes "Frontiers of reconciliation." This reframing moves from the imagery of direct combat to the concept of exploring new territories in peace-making, emphasizing the pioneering work of bridging divides and healing relationships.

272. "Frontiers of warfare" becomes "Horizons of peace." Instead of marking the boundaries of conflict, this phrase suggests looking towards the future possibilities for harmony, highlighting the forward momentum towards peaceful coexistence.

273. "Frontline of war" becomes "Forefront of reconciliation." This reframing moves from a position of direct conflict to leading the charge towards mending divides, emphasizing proactive efforts in healing and bringing together opposing sides.

274. "Futility of resistance" becomes "Power of persistence."

Instead of suggesting that opposition is pointless, this phrase champions the effectiveness of continued effort and determination, promoting the idea that steadfastness can lead to meaningful change.

275. "Garrison mentality" becomes "Community spirit." This reframing moves from a defensive, fortress-like mindset to one of openness and collective well-being, promoting the idea of strength in unity and communal support.

276. "Garrison of fear" becomes "Sanctuary of courage." This reframing suggests transforming a stronghold of anxiety into a refuge of bravery, promoting the idea that within each person lies a safe space where they can find their inner strength.

277. "Gathering storm clouds" becomes "Cultivating a climate of change." Instead of impending turmoil, this reframing suggests actively working to create an environment conducive to positive transformations, emphasizing proactive engagement with challenges.

278. "Ghosts of battles past" becomes "Guides for future peace." It changes the narrative from being haunted by previous conflicts to learning from them, promoting the idea that history can instruct and lead the way to avoiding future strife.

279. "Ghosts of the past" becomes "Guides for the future." Instead of being haunted by previous events, this phrase suggests using historical experiences as lessons to inform and improve future decisions, emphasizing learning from history.

280. "Ghosts of the past" becomes "Guides for the future." This reframing suggests that memories and experiences from the past can serve as valuable lessons that inform and direct future actions, promoting the idea of learning from history.

281. "Give one's life for freedom" becomes "Live every day for freedom." It emphasizes the daily pursuit of liberty and self-determination, inspiring continuous action towards the goal of

freedom.

282. "Going down fighting" becomes "Rising up with resilience." It changes the narrative from a defeatist attitude to one of bouncing back and overcoming adversity, focusing on the strength and adaptability of the human spirit.

283. "Going down with the ship" becomes "Steering towards safer shores." It reframes a hopeless situation into a journey toward safety and stability, emphasizing resilience and the pursuit of secure havens.

284. "Grave consequences" becomes "Valuable outcomes." This reframing suggests that the results of our actions, even when serious, can be beneficial and instructive, emphasizing the potential for learning and improvement.

285. "Grievances held" becomes "Forgiveness offered." It transforms the narrative from clinging to past wrongs to extending the olive branch, promoting the healing power of forgiveness as a foundation for building a peaceful future together.

286. "Grim forecast" becomes "Hopeful outlook." It changes the narrative from a bleak prediction to an optimistic anticipation of the future, highlighting the importance of maintaining a positive perspective.

287. "Grim realities" becomes "Brighter possibilities." It shifts from focusing on harsh truths to envisioning hopeful futures, emphasizing the potential for positive outcomes even in difficult circumstances.

288. "Grim realities" becomes "Brighter truths." It changes the focus from harsh conditions to the enlightening realizations that can emerge, emphasizing the clarity and insight gained through facing tough situations.

289. "Grim reaper's call" becomes "Life's inviting call." This shifts the narrative from an ominous summoning to an

enticing invitation to engage more deeply with life, emphasizing opportunity and invitation over finality.

290. "Grim reminders" becomes "Hopeful symbols." Instead of objects or memories that evoke pain, this phrase suggests signs that inspire optimism, emphasizing the potential for reminders to serve as beacons of hope.

291. "Grinding to a halt" becomes "Pausing for perspective." This reframing suggests that a stop is not an end but a moment to reflect and reassess, promoting the idea that pauses can lead to better-informed actions.

292. "Ground down by strife" becomes "Lifted by solidarity." Instead of being diminished by conflict, this phrase envisions being elevated by unity and support, emphasizing the uplifting power of collective strength.

293. "Ground zero" becomes "Foundation for renewal." It shifts from a site of devastation to the starting point for rebuilding and growth, emphasizing the potential for new beginnings and positive change following destruction.

294. "Ground zero" becomes "Foundation stone." Instead of a site of devastation, this reframing envisions the starting point for building something new and enduring, highlighting the potential for reconstruction and progress.

295. "Ground zero" becomes "Grounds for growth." This reframing transforms a site of destruction into a fertile area for development, emphasizing the potential for new beginnings and positive change.

296. "Grounds for battle" becomes "Grounds for agreement." It changes the narrative from preparing for conflict to preparing for consensus, highlighting the potential for finding common ground and shared solutions.

297. "Grounds for war" becomes "Reasons for peace." This reframing suggests that the motivations for conflict can be

transformed into justifications for harmony, highlighting the potential to redirect energies towards peaceful outcomes.

298. "Grounds of defeat" becomes "Lessons of resilience." Instead of a place where one is overcome by failure, this phrase suggests a learning environment where resilience is built through overcoming challenges.

299. "Guarded against all threats" becomes "Open to all possibilities." This phrase suggests a posture of receptiveness and optimism, rather than defensiveness, promoting an environment where opportunities can be embraced.

300. "Guarded hearts" becomes "Open hearts." This reframing suggests moving from protecting oneself from emotional exposure to embracing vulnerability and connection, emphasizing the power of openness in healing and relationships.

301. "Guardian of the past" becomes "Caretaker of the future." It shifts the focus from protecting what has been to nurturing what will be, highlighting the role of stewardship in shaping a positive legacy.

302. "Guarding against threats" becomes "Welcoming new understandings." Instead of being defensive, this phrase encourages openness to new perspectives, promoting the idea that perceived threats can lead to greater insight and mutual respect.

303. "Guarding one's position" becomes "Sharing one's perspective." Moving from a defensive posture to one of openness, this phrase promotes the exchange of ideas and mutual respect for differing viewpoints.

304. "Guerilla warfare" becomes "Guerilla growth." It transforms the concept of irregular and unexpected combat into the idea of rapid and surprising development, emphasizing adaptability and innovation.

305. "Guerilla warfare" becomes "Guerilla peacemaking." This

reframing changes the narrative from irregular fighting to unconventional efforts for peace, emphasizing creative and grassroots approaches to resolving conflict.

306. "Guerrilla tactics" becomes "Grassroots initiatives." Instead of irregular warfare methods, this phrase highlights community-driven efforts to effect change, promoting the power of collective action from the ground up for positive outcomes.

307. "Guerrilla tactics" becomes "Innovative strategies." It changes the narrative from unconventional warfare to creative problem-solving, highlighting the adaptability and ingenuity required to navigate complex challenges.

308. "Guerrilla warfare" becomes "Guerrilla gardening." It changes the narrative from irregular and surprise tactics in conflict to the act of planting and cultivating life in unexpected places, highlighting creative and positive interventions in neglected or challenging environments.

309. "Guerrilla warfare" becomes "Guerrilla growth." It changes the narrative from irregular combat to unexpected and innovative development, highlighting the adaptability and creativity that can flourish in challenging conditions.

310. "Harbinger of doom" becomes "Herald of dawn." Instead of signaling impending disaster, this phrase suggests announcing the arrival of new beginnings and opportunities, emphasizing the cyclical nature of endings and starts.

311. "Hardened by hostility" becomes "Softened by compassion." It shifts from becoming tough in the face of aggression to becoming empathetic, promoting the idea that kindness and understanding are powerful responses to animosity.

312. "Harsh battleground" becomes "Fertile ground for peace." This reframing suggests that even the most difficult and contentious areas can become places where peace takes root and grows, emphasizing the transformative potential of

reconciliation.

313. "Harsh judgments" becomes "Paths to understanding." This reframing suggests that criticism can lead to deeper comprehension and empathy, promoting the idea that feedback is an opportunity for personal and relational growth.

314. "Harsh realities" becomes "Invitations to innovate." This reframing moves from the grimness of certain truths to the encouragement to create solutions, promoting the idea that challenges invite creativity and ingenuity.

315. "Haunted by regret" becomes "Guided by reflection." Instead of being tormented by thoughts of what could have been, this phrase suggests using past decisions as a source of insight for future choices, promoting thoughtful contemplation.

316. "Havoc of war" becomes "Harmony of coexistence." Instead of chaos and destruction, this phrase envisions a state of balance and peaceful living, emphasizing the potential for diverse groups to live together in mutual respect.

317. "Heart of darkness" becomes "Light of compassion." Instead of an inner core of despair or evil, this phrase suggests a center filled with empathy and kindness, highlighting the human capacity for understanding and benevolence even in the toughest times.

318. "Heart of darkness" becomes "Source of light." Instead of a core of despair or malevolence, this phrase envisions a center from which hope and goodness emanate, promoting the idea that even in difficulty, there can be a guiding positivity.

319. "Heavy artillery" becomes "Heavy support." It changes the focus from weapons of war to robust systems of assistance and aid, highlighting the importance of backing and resources in overcoming challenges.

320. "Heavy bombardment" becomes "Abundant support." Moving from the imagery of relentless attacks to the provision

of generous assistance, this phrase promotes the idea of overwhelming aid and encouragement.

321. "Heavy burden of sorrow" becomes "Lightness of shared solace." Instead of carrying grief alone, this phrase envisions the ease that comes from communal support and shared healing, highlighting the comfort found in togetherness.

322. "Heavy casualties" becomes "Valuable lessons." It changes the narrative from loss to learning, highlighting that even in the most challenging circumstances, there are important insights to be gained that can guide future actions.

323. "Historical conflicts" becomes "Future collaborations." Instead of dwelling on historical disputes, this phrase looks forward to potential joint ventures, emphasizing the opportunities for cooperative projects that can benefit both nations and their peoples.

324. "Hold the fort at all costs" becomes "Nurture the garden for all." It shifts the focus from defensive warfare to the collaborative cultivation of a community, highlighting the shared responsibility for growth and prosperity.

325. "Holding hostages" becomes "Hosting dialogues." Moving from a situation of captivity and control to one of open communication and exchange, this phrase promotes the power of conversation over coercion.

326. "Holding the fort" becomes "Opening the home." It changes the narrative from a defensive stance to one of hospitality and community, promoting the idea of welcoming others and sharing spaces.

327. "Holding the line" becomes "Extending a bridge." Instead of maintaining a rigid stance, this reframing suggests reaching out to connect with others, symbolizing efforts to overcome barriers and find commonality.

328. "Holding the line" becomes "Holding out hope." Instead

of maintaining a defensive position, this phrase suggests keeping faith in positive outcomes, promoting an optimistic stance in the face of challenges.

329. "Hostile environment" becomes "Nurturing atmosphere." It changes the narrative from a place of aggression to one of care and growth, promoting the idea that even the most challenging environments can be transformed into supportive spaces.

330. "Hostile takeover" becomes "Friendly merger." This reframing suggests a shift from aggression and dominance to collaboration and mutual agreement, emphasizing the benefits of cooperative approaches in conflict resolution.

331. "Hostile territory" becomes "Lands of learning." This reframing suggests that even in environments of opposition, there is much to learn, promoting the idea that every challenge is an educational journey.

332. "Impasse of disagreement" becomes "Gateway to consensus." It shifts from a deadlock to an opening for agreement, highlighting the opportunity for dialogue and compromise that can arise when opposing views are expressed.

333. "Impending doom" becomes "Impending growth." Instead of a sense of unavoidable disaster, this phrase envisions a near certainty of personal development, highlighting the potential for positive change on the horizon.

334. "Impenetrable defenses" becomes "Open channels for dialogue." Instead of barriers that prevent communication, this phrase envisions pathways that facilitate open and honest exchanges, promoting the idea that understanding can break down even the toughest walls.

335. "Impenetrable defenses" becomes "Welcoming embraces." This reframing moves from the imagery of barriers to the warmth of inclusion, emphasizing the power of openness and the strength found in unity.

336. "In the heat of battle" becomes "In the warmth of camaraderie." It reframes the intensity of conflict into the comforting presence of fellowship, focusing on the supportive and nurturing aspects of human connection.

337. "In the heat of battle" becomes "In the warmth of unity." Instead of the intensity of conflict, this phrase suggests the comfort and strength found in solidarity, emphasizing the positive aspects of coming together.

338. "In the jaws of defeat" becomes "In the embrace of opportunity." It shifts from the brink of failure to being held by potential success, emphasizing the possibilities that arise even in challenging times.

339. "In the line of duty" becomes "In the pursuit of service." This reframing focuses on the noble aspects of duty, highlighting the commitment to serving a greater good and the well-being of others.

340. "In the line of duty" becomes "In the pursuit of service." Instead of a phrase that often implies risk or sacrifice, this reframing emphasizes the noble aspects of serving others and contributing to the greater good.

341. "In the line of duty" becomes "In the service of life." This reframing suggests that actions taken are not just obligations but are contributions to the vitality and well-being of others, emphasizing service and care.

342. "In the line of fire" becomes "In the light of hope." Instead of being in a dangerous position, this reframing suggests being in a place where one is guided and inspired by hope, emphasizing the positive outlook that can lead through adversity.

343. "In the line of fire" becomes "In the line of hope." This phrase suggests that even in dangerous or challenging situations, there is a guiding light of hope that can lead to safer and more positive outcomes.

344. "In the midst of chaos" becomes "At the center of creativity." This phrase suggests that within disorder lies the potential for creative breakthroughs, encouraging a search for innovation in the face of confusion.

345. "In the shadow of conflict" becomes "In the light of resolution." This phrase suggests moving out of the darkness of ongoing strife into the brightness of conflict resolution, emphasizing the clarity and hope that come with finding solutions.

346. "In the shadow of war" becomes "In the light of reconciliation." This reframing moves from the darkness associated with conflict to the brightness of coming together and healing, emphasizing the positive outcomes of peace efforts.

347. "In the trenches" becomes "On the bridge to understanding." This phrase suggests moving from a defensive position to a connective pathway, emphasizing efforts to reach across divides and foster mutual comprehension.

348. "In the trenches" becomes "On the bridge." Moving away from the imagery of being dug into battle positions, this phrase suggests standing on a structure that connects and facilitates crossing over obstacles.

349. "In the trenches" becomes "On the peaks." It shifts from being in a confined, low place to standing atop high ground with a broad perspective, emphasizing the advantage of seeing situations from a higher vantage point.

350. "In the trenches" becomes "On the peaks." This reframing suggests moving from a position of entrenchment and defense to one of overview and perspective, emphasizing a higher vantage point for broader understanding.

351. "Insurgency" becomes "Resurgence." Instead of rebellion or uprising, this phrase suggests a powerful recovery or revival, promoting the idea of bouncing back stronger and more unified.

352. "Insurgents" becomes "Change agents." This reframing suggests viewing those who resist or rebel not as threats but as individuals driving transformation, emphasizing their potential role in societal progress.

353. "Insurmountable barriers" becomes "Navigable obstacles." Instead of viewing challenges as impossible to overcome, this phrase suggests that with creativity and perseverance, obstacles can be managed and crossed, highlighting the journey towards achievement.

354. "Insurmountable odds" becomes "Mountains of opportunity." It shifts from viewing challenges as impossible to overcome to seeing them as opportunities for achievement and growth, emphasizing the potential for success through perseverance and innovation.

355. "Invasion of privacy" becomes "Celebration of individuality." It shifts from an act of intrusion to an acknowledgment and respect for personal uniqueness, emphasizing the value of each person's space and identity.

356. "Invasion of privacy" becomes "Opportunity for boundary-setting." This reframing suggests that intrusions can serve as catalysts for clarifying and asserting personal limits, promoting the development of healthier relationships.

357. "Iron grip of war" becomes "Gentle hands of peace." It changes the narrative from the harsh control of conflict to the nurturing touch of peace, highlighting the care and tenderness involved in healing and reconciliation.

358. "Islands of despair" becomes "Continents of hope." This reframing moves from isolated spots of sorrow to vast expanses of optimism, emphasizing the abundance of hope and the wide-reaching potential for positive change.

359. "Islands of isolation" becomes "Bridges of community." Instead of being separated by barriers, this phrase suggests

connections that foster unity and support, promoting the idea of overcoming isolation through communal bonds.

360. "Islands of isolation" becomes "Bridges of connection." This reframing moves from solitary separation to structures that facilitate unity, emphasizing the importance of reaching out and establishing bonds.

361. "Isolated in adversity" becomes "Connected through shared experiences." Instead of focusing on solitude during tough times, this phrase emphasizes the bonds formed through common struggles, promoting a sense of community and support.

362. "Isolated in adversity" becomes "United in recovery." Instead of being alone in hardship, this phrase suggests a collective journey towards healing, emphasizing the strength found in shared experiences and mutual support.

363. "Isolated in struggle" becomes "United in resilience." This reframing moves from a sense of solitary hardship to a recognition of shared strength and endurance, highlighting the communal support found in facing difficulties together.

364. "Isolation of enmity" becomes "Embrace of fellowship." Instead of being separated by animosity, this phrase suggests coming together in a spirit of camaraderie, emphasizing the warmth and strength found in friendship and shared purpose.

365. "Isolation" becomes "Integration." This reframing suggests moving from separation to creating inclusive communities, highlighting the benefits of cultural exchange and shared experiences in fostering understanding and unity.

366. "Jaded by disappointment" becomes "Renewed by hope." It shifts from a state of disillusionment to a rejuvenation of optimism, emphasizing the ability to find new reasons for hope even after experiencing letdowns.

367. "Jagged edges of conflict" becomes "Smooth contours of consensus." This reframing moves from the sharpness of

disagreement to the gentle curves of agreement, promoting the idea that finding common ground can lead to smoother interactions.

368. "Jagged edges of war" becomes "Smooth paths of reconciliation." Instead of focusing on the harsh and painful aspects of conflict, this phrase envisions the journey towards making amends as a process that becomes easier and more harmonious over time.

369. "Jagged rifts" becomes "Seamless bonds." This reframing moves from sharp divisions to smooth connections, promoting the idea that relationships can be mended and strengthened, creating a more unified whole.

370. "Jagged scars" becomes "Lines of learning." It shifts from marks of past wounds to symbols of lessons learned and wisdom gained, emphasizing the value of experiences that shape and teach us.

371. "Jaws of defeat" becomes "Embrace of opportunity." It shifts from the imagery of being consumed by failure to being held in a space where new possibilities are presented, promoting the idea that setbacks can lead to new paths.

372. "Jingoism" becomes "Empathy." It shifts from nationalistic fervor to a compassionate understanding of the other side, promoting the idea that seeing the world from another's perspective can dissolve animosity and build bridges.

373. "Jungle of dangers" becomes "Garden of opportunities." It transforms the perception of a threatening environment into a nurturing space where possibilities can be cultivated, emphasizing growth and potential amidst challenges.

374. "Jungle of dangers" becomes "Garden of opportunities." It transforms the imagery from a place fraught with threats to a space abundant with chances for growth, highlighting the potential for positive outcomes amidst risks.

375. "Killed in action" becomes "Inspired to action." It shifts from the finality of death to the motivation to act, suggesting that the sacrifices made can serve as a powerful impetus for others to work towards meaningful change.

376. "Killing fields" becomes "Healing fields." Instead of areas marked by death and destruction, this phrase envisions spaces dedicated to recovery and restoration, emphasizing the potential for places of sorrow to transform into sources of solace and healing.

377. "Killing time" becomes "Cherishing moments." It changes the narrative from idly passing time to actively appreciating and making the most of every moment, emphasizing the value of being present and engaged.

378. "Killing time" becomes "Cultivating time." It shifts from idly passing moments to actively making the most of them, emphasizing intentional engagement and productivity.

379. "Knee-deep in adversity" becomes "Elevated by challenge." Instead of being submerged in difficulties, this phrase suggests rising above them, emphasizing the elevation in perspective and character that comes from facing and overcoming obstacles.

380. "Knee-deep in adversity" becomes "Waist-high in resilience." This reframing moves from being submerged in difficulties to standing strong amidst them, emphasizing the depth of one's resilience in challenging times.

381. "Knee-deep in conflict" becomes "Eye-level with solutions." This reframing moves from being submerged in problems to looking directly at potential answers, promoting an active and solution-focused approach to resolving disputes.

382. "Knee-deep in trouble" becomes "Ankle-deep in solutions." Instead of being overwhelmed by problems, this phrase suggests standing amidst emerging answers, emphasizing the readiness to act on potential fixes.

383. "Knocked down by life" becomes "Lifted by learning." Instead of focusing on the fall, this phrase emphasizes the uplifting effect of gaining knowledge and insight from life's challenges, promoting a positive outlook on personal growth.

384. "Knocked down" becomes "Set up for a comeback." This reframing changes the narrative from defeat to the preparation for a resurgence, promoting the idea that falling down is often just a step in the process of rising stronger.

385. "Knots of tension" becomes "Bonds of understanding." It transforms the tight, uncomfortable binds of conflict into connections that are strengthened by empathy and mutual comprehension, highlighting the transformative power of truly listening and relating to one another.

386. "Kremlin's stance" and "Kyiv's position" become "Common ground." This reframing moves from focusing on the differences between the two capitals to finding areas of agreement, emphasizing the potential for shared interests that can serve as a basis for dialogue.

387. "Labyrinth of conflict" becomes "Maze of understanding." This reframing suggests that navigating disagreements is not a trap but a journey towards comprehension, emphasizing the potential for discovery and insight within complex issues.

388. "Labyrinth of strife" becomes "Pathway of concord." It transforms a complex network of conflict into a straightforward route to agreement, highlighting the potential for navigating through discord to reach a place of harmony.

389. "Labyrinths of misunderstanding" becomes "Clearings of clarity." This reframing suggests moving from confusing and complicated disagreements to open spaces where things are seen more clearly, promoting the importance of transparency and direct communication.

390. "Landscape of despair" becomes "Horizon of hope." Instead

of a view marred by hopelessness, this reframing presents a vista filled with optimism for the future, highlighting the potential for positive change and the dawn of a new era of peace.

391. "<u>Last man standing</u>" becomes "<u>First step forward.</u>" Instead of focusing on survival after conflict, this phrase suggests the beginning of collective progress, highlighting the opportunity to lead the way in healing and rebuilding.

392. "<u>Last stand of person</u>" becomes "<u>Lasting stand for peace.</u>" By focusing on peace rather than a final act of defiance, this phrase promotes the idea of enduring efforts towards harmony and the long-term benefits of conflict resolution.

393. "<u>Last stand</u>" becomes "<u>New beginning.</u>" It changes the narrative from a final, desperate defense to the first step towards a fresh start and new opportunities, promoting optimism and the potential for renewal.

394. "<u>Last stand</u>" becomes "<u>New beginning.</u>" This reframing suggests that what might seem like a final defense can actually mark the start of a new chapter of opportunities, promoting hope and the potential for renewal.

395. "<u>Lay down arms</u>" becomes "<u>Lift up hearts.</u>" This reframing moves from the cessation of fighting to the elevation of spirits, promoting the idea of raising morale and fostering goodwill.

396. "<u>Lay down one's life</u>" becomes "<u>Uphold life's value.</u>" This reframing reinforces the intrinsic worth of every individual, advocating for actions that respect and preserve life.

397. "<u>Lay down your life</u>" becomes "<u>Enrich others' lives.</u>" It shifts from the ultimate sacrifice to contributing positively to the lives of others, highlighting the impact one can have through acts of service and kindness.

398. "<u>Lay siege to</u>" becomes "<u>Build bridges to.</u>" This shifts from an act of aggression to an act of construction, emphasizing efforts to connect and understand rather than to isolate and conquer.

399. "Lay siege to" becomes "Cultivate around." Moving from an act of aggression to one of nurturing growth, this phrase promotes the idea of surrounding a problem with care and attention to foster positive outcomes.

400. "Lay waste to" becomes "Cultivate anew." This reframing suggests that instead of destroying, there is an opportunity to nurture and grow, emphasizing the potential for positive creation following destruction.

401. "Laying down one's weapons" becomes "Raising up one's voice." This suggests transitioning from armed conflict to active dialogue, emphasizing the power of communication over the use of force.

402. "Licking wounds" becomes "Healing and growing." This phrase moves from a focus on injury and pain to the process of recovery and personal development, highlighting the journey towards wholeness.

403. "Lines drawn in the sand" becomes "Paths paved for walking together." Instead of marking divisions, this phrase suggests creating routes that encourage joint progress, emphasizing collaboration and shared journeys.

404. "Lines in the sand" becomes "Bridges over barriers." This reframing moves from drawing divisions to building connections, emphasizing efforts to overcome obstacles and unite people.

405. "Lingering in the aftermath" becomes "Moving towards renewal." Instead of remaining in the shadow of events, this phrase suggests progressing into a phase of rejuvenation and growth, emphasizing the dynamic nature of recovery.

406. "Lingering in the aftermath" becomes "Propelling into action." Instead of remaining in the shadow of events, this reframing suggests using the past as a catalyst for proactive steps forward, promoting a dynamic and purposeful response to adversity.

407. "Locked in combat" becomes "Engaged in cooperation." Shifting from confrontation to collaboration, this phrase highlights the benefits of working together towards common goals, promoting unity and shared success.

408. "Looming shadows of doubt" becomes "Rising sun of certainty." It transforms the image of encroaching uncertainty into the promise of clear, illuminating assurance, promoting the idea that clarity often follows periods of questioning.

409. "Losing battles" becomes "Learning opportunities." Instead of focusing on defeat, this phrase highlights each setback as a chance to gain valuable insights, promoting a mindset of continuous learning and adaptation.

410. "Losing ground" becomes "Planting seeds for new growth." This phrase reframes a setback as an opportunity to lay the groundwork for future success, focusing on the potential for progress and development.

411. "Losing the battle" becomes "Embracing the lesson." Instead of focusing on defeat, this phrase highlights the value of learning and growth that comes from challenges, suggesting that every setback is an opportunity for development.

412. "Losses mourned" becomes "Lives celebrated." Instead of focusing solely on what has been lost, this phrase encourages celebrating the lives and contributions of individuals, fostering a culture of appreciation and respect for all affected by the conflict.

413. "Lost cause" becomes "Found purpose." This reframing moves from a sense of hopelessness to discovering a meaningful direction, highlighting the potential for clarity and motivation even in challenging situations.

414. "Lost causes" becomes "Hidden opportunities." It transforms the notion of hopeless endeavors into chances for uncovering potential and making unexpected gains, promoting optimism and the search for silver linings.

415. "Lost in darkness" becomes "Guided by starlight." Instead of wandering without direction, this phrase suggests using the faintest sources of light as guidance, promoting the idea that even in the darkest times, there is direction and hope.

416. "Lost in darkness" becomes "Guided by stars." Instead of despairing in the absence of light, this phrase suggests using points of hope and guidance to find one's way, promoting optimism and direction.

417. "Lost in the darkness" becomes "Seeking the dawn." Instead of being trapped in despair, this reframing speaks to the active search for the first light of hope and new beginnings.

418. "Lost in the fog of war" becomes "Found in the clarity of peace." Instead of being disoriented by conflict, this phrase promotes finding direction and purpose in efforts toward peace, emphasizing resolution and clarity.

419. "Lost in the fog of war" becomes "Guided by the beacon of hope." Instead of being disoriented by conflict, this phrase envisions a guiding light leading the way out, emphasizing the importance of maintaining hope and direction amidst turmoil.

420. "Lost in the shadows" becomes "Guided by the light." It changes the narrative from being obscured and hidden to seeking out and following beacons of guidance and enlightenment, emphasizing the journey towards clarity.

421. "Lost in translation" becomes "Found in understanding." Instead of focusing on miscommunication, this phrase highlights the opportunity to reach deeper levels of comprehension and connection through the effort to clarify and empathize.

422. "Lost to time" becomes "Immortalized in memory." This reframing shifts the focus from being forgotten to being eternally remembered, emphasizing the enduring impact one has on the lives of others through cherished memories.

423. "Man the barricades" becomes "Open the gates of dialogue." Instead of preparing for siege, this phrase encourages opening pathways to communication, symbolizing an invitation to understanding and cooperation.

424. "Man the barricades" becomes "Open the gates." This reframing suggests dismantling defenses to welcome new ideas and people, emphasizing inclusivity and the benefits of embracing change and cooperation.

425. "March of conquest" becomes "Parade of progress." This reframing changes the narrative from domination to advancement, focusing on celebrating achievements and forward movement as a community.

426. "March of death" becomes "March of life." This reframing moves from a procession associated with loss and ending to one that celebrates existence and continuity, promoting a focus on the vibrancy and potential of life.

427. "March of doom" becomes "Stride towards solutions." Instead of a procession toward inevitable destruction, this phrase suggests purposeful movement towards resolving issues, highlighting the proactive nature of seeking positive outcomes.

428. "March of vengeance" becomes "March of forgiveness." Instead of seeking retribution, this phrase suggests a collective movement towards understanding and pardoning, highlighting the power of forgiveness to heal and restore peace.

429. "March of vengeance" becomes "March of virtue." Instead of seeking retribution, this phrase suggests advancing with moral excellence and integrity, promoting actions guided by high ethical standards.

430. "March to war" becomes "March to progress." This phrase suggests moving forward with purpose and improvement in mind, rather than advancing towards conflict, highlighting a journey of collective advancement.

431. "March to war" becomes "Stride towards peace." This reframing moves from advancing towards conflict to progressing with purpose towards peaceful resolutions, emphasizing deliberate and positive movement.

432. "Marching into battle" becomes "Marching towards progress." This reframing suggests a collective movement not towards conflict but towards societal improvement and advancement, highlighting the importance of shared goals and development.

433. "Marching into darkness" becomes "Journeying towards enlightenment." It shifts from a grim advance into uncertainty to a hopeful progression towards understanding and awareness, promoting the idea of growth through adversity.

434. "Marching into darkness" becomes "Stepping into the dawn." This reframing suggests moving not towards obscurity but towards the promise of a new day and the fresh opportunities it brings, highlighting optimism and renewal.

435. "Marching into the storm" becomes "Guiding towards the calm." Instead of moving into turmoil, this phrase encourages leading others to peace and tranquility, highlighting the role of guidance and foresight.

436. "Marching orders" becomes "Paths of discovery." Instead of following commands that lead to predictable outcomes, this phrase encourages exploration and the joy of discovering new possibilities.

437. "Marching to the beat of war drums" becomes "Dancing to the rhythm of life." It shifts from mobilization for conflict to celebrating existence and joy, promoting a life-affirming approach to communal and individual actions.

438. "Marching to war" becomes "Advancing to understanding." This reframing moves from mobilization for conflict to progression towards mutual comprehension, highlighting the

journey towards empathy and shared insights.

439. "<u>Martial conflict</u>" becomes "<u>Civic accord.</u>" Moving from a focus on military disputes to a focus on civil agreement, this phrase promotes the idea of resolving issues through democratic and peaceful means.

440. "<u>Martial law</u>" becomes "<u>Civil harmony.</u>" Instead of the strict control of military rule, this phrase suggests the peaceful order of a society working together in cooperation, emphasizing the preference for civil solutions.

441. "<u>Martyr for the cause</u>" becomes "<u>Champion for the cause.</u>" It shifts from sacrifice to active advocacy, suggesting a life dedicated to advancing a cause without the need for self-sacrifice.

442. "<u>Martyrs of the cause</u>" becomes "<u>Champions of the cause.</u>" Instead of focusing on sacrifice, this phrase celebrates active advocacy and dedication, highlighting the positive impact of standing for a belief or purpose.

443. "<u>Meet one's maker</u>" becomes "<u>Meet one's potential.</u>" It inspires individuals to strive for their best, suggesting that life's challenges are opportunities for growth and self-realization.

444. "<u>Military engagements</u>" becomes "<u>Peaceful encounters.</u>" It transforms the concept of military confrontations into opportunities for non-violent interactions, highlighting the importance of choosing dialogue and diplomacy over force.

445. "<u>Military occupation</u>" becomes "<u>Civic engagement.</u>" Instead of control through force, this phrase envisions active participation and involvement in community affairs, emphasizing the importance of collaboration and shared responsibility in governance.

446. "<u>Minefield of danger</u>" becomes "<u>Field of opportunities.</u>" It transforms a perilous situation into a landscape rich with potential, highlighting the ability to navigate through risks to find possibilities for success.

447. "Minefields of the past" becomes "Gardens of the future." It transforms the image of dangerous remnants from previous conflicts into spaces for growth and nurturing, emphasizing the potential for healing and new beginnings.

448. "Minefields" becomes "Fields of discovery." It transforms the idea of dangerous obstacles into opportunities for careful exploration and finding new paths, emphasizing cautious progress and the rewards of perseverance.

449. "Mines of mistrust" becomes "Fields of fidelity." Instead of areas fraught with suspicion and betrayal, this phrase envisions expanses rich with loyalty and trust, emphasizing the potential to cultivate strong, reliable relationships.

450. "Mired in combat" becomes "Elevated by collaboration." Instead of being stuck in a state of fighting, this phrase suggests rising to work jointly on solutions, highlighting the benefits of teamwork and shared problem-solving.

451. "Mired in conflict" becomes "Elevated by understanding." Moving from being stuck in disputes to rising above them through comprehension and empathy, this reframing promotes the resolution of conflicts through deeper insight into their causes.

452. "Mired in defeat" becomes "Rising to challenge." This reframing moves from a sense of being stuck in failure to the act of confronting and overcoming difficulties, emphasizing resilience and the courage to face adversity.

453. "Mired in the past" becomes "Anchored by history." It shifts from being stuck to being stabilized and informed by past experiences, promoting the idea that history provides a foundation from which to move forward wisely.

454. "Mobilize for war" becomes "Mobilize for well-being." Instead of rallying forces for battle, this reframing suggests rallying resources for the health and happiness of the community, promoting proactive care and support.

455. "Muted aspirations" becomes "Amplified dreams." This reframing changes the narrative from subdued hopes to loudly proclaimed ambitions, promoting the idea that our desires and goals deserve to be heard and pursued with vigor.

456. "Muted by fear" becomes "Voiced by bravery." It transforms the silence caused by fear into the expression enabled by courage, highlighting the power of overcoming fear to speak out and take action.

457. "Muted by oppression" becomes "Amplified by expression." This reframing changes the narrative from being silenced to finding one's voice and speaking out, highlighting the power of self-expression and advocacy.

458. "Muted voices" becomes "Emerging chorus." It transforms the narrative from silenced individuals to a collective voice growing stronger, highlighting the power of unity and shared expression.

459. "Nationalistic fervor" becomes "Cultural appreciation." This reframing shifts from aggressive patriotism to a mutual respect and admiration for each other's culture, promoting the idea that cultural exchange can lead to a deeper understanding and friendship.

460. "Neutral ground" becomes "Common soil." Instead of a place lacking affiliation, this phrase envisions a shared foundation for growth and collaboration, promoting the idea of unity and mutual support.

461. "Neutralize the threat" becomes "Harmonize the interests." Instead of eliminating opposition, this phrase suggests aligning differing needs and desires to achieve balance, promoting the idea of reconciliation and mutual benefit.

462. "Nightmares of the past" becomes "Dreams of the future." It shifts from being tormented by previous traumas to being inspired by visions of what can be, promoting an outlook that is

forward-looking and aspirational.

463. "No end in sight" becomes "Endless possibilities." This reframing changes the narrative from a lack of conclusion to an abundance of opportunities, emphasizing the boundless potential that lies ahead.

464. "No man's land" becomes "A land of potential." This reframing transforms a barren, contested space into an area ripe with possibilities for development and cooperation, highlighting the untapped opportunities that lie within.

465. "No man's land" becomes "Common ground." This reframing changes a place of division and desolation into a shared space for collaboration and mutual understanding, promoting the idea of finding unity in previously contested areas.

466. "No man's land" becomes "Common ground." This shifts from a place of isolation and desolation to a space where shared interests and cooperation can be cultivated, emphasizing the potential for unity.

467. "No man's land" becomes "Every community's garden." It transforms a place of exclusion and desolation into a shared space for growth and nurturing, promoting the idea of communal care and regeneration.

468. "No man's land" becomes "Every person's bridge." This reframing transforms a place of separation into a connector for all, emphasizing inclusivity and the potential for shared spaces to unite.

469. "No man's land" becomes "Every person's bridge." It transforms a place of exclusion into a connector for all, emphasizing inclusivity and the potential for shared spaces to unite.

470. "No man's land" becomes "Every person's peace park." This reframing moves from a place devoid of life and ownership to a shared space dedicated to tranquility and communal enjoyment,

highlighting the transformation of contested areas into zones of harmony.

471. "<u>No man's land</u>" becomes "<u>Everyone's garden.</u>" It transforms a barren, disputed area into a shared space for cultivation and nourishment, emphasizing community and the shared stewardship of resources.

472. "<u>No man's land</u>" becomes "<u>Land of possibilities.</u>" It transforms a place characterized by absence and desolation into a space ripe for creation and growth, highlighting the untapped potential waiting to be explored.

473. "<u>No man's land</u>" becomes "<u>Shared space.</u>" It transforms a place of exclusion and danger into an area of commonality and safety, promoting the idea of territories that bring people together rather than keep them apart.

474. "<u>No peace in sight</u>" becomes "<u>Horizons of harmony.</u>" It transforms a bleak outlook into one of hopeful prospects, promoting the idea that peace is a journey with promising destinations on the horizon.

475. "<u>No retreat, no surrender</u>" becomes "<u>Always advance, always unite.</u>" Instead of a refusal to give ground, this phrase encourages continual progress and the strengthening of bonds, highlighting a positive, forward-moving, and collaborative approach.

476. "<u>No retreat, no surrender</u>" becomes "<u>No giving up on peace.</u>" The focus here is on the relentless pursuit of peace rather than a dogged commitment to stand one's ground in battle, promoting the idea of continuous efforts towards reconciliation.

477. "<u>No surrender</u>" becomes "<u>Yes to compromise.</u>" It changes the narrative from a refusal to give in to an affirmation of finding middle ground, highlighting the value of negotiation and mutual agreement.

478. "<u>No-man's land</u>" becomes "<u>Common ground.</u>" This

reframing moves from a place of isolation and division to a shared space where mutual interests and understanding can be found, promoting unity and cooperation.

479. "No-man's land" becomes "Common ground." It transforms a place of isolation and contention into a shared space for collaboration and mutual respect, emphasizing the potential for unity and shared purpose.

480. "No-man's land" becomes "Every person's bridge." This reframing moves from a place of desolation and division to a connector for all, emphasizing inclusivity and the potential to unite disparate sides.

481. "Noxious atmosphere of hostility" becomes "Invigorating air of cooperation." Instead of an environment filled with animosity, this phrase envisions a space where collaborative efforts are revitalizing and productive, promoting the benefits of working together.

482. "Noxious fumes of hostility" becomes "Refreshing breeze of amity." Instead of toxic and harmful air, this phrase envisions a revitalizing wind, emphasizing the invigorating and healing effects of friendly and kind interactions.

483. "Occupied territories" becomes "Communities of collaboration." Instead of areas under control, this phrase suggests spaces where cooperative efforts flourish, promoting the idea of working together for common goals.

484. "Occupied territory" becomes "Shared land." Instead of a region under control, this phrase envisions an area jointly inhabited and managed, promoting the idea of cooperative stewardship.

485. "Oceans of sorrow" becomes "Rivers of resilience." This reframing moves from vast, overwhelming grief to the dynamic flow of strength and perseverance, highlighting the continuous journey of recovery and adaptation.

486. "One's final moments" becomes "One's lasting impact." This reframing shifts the focus from the end of life to the enduring influence one has, emphasizing the legacy left behind and its ongoing effect.

487. "Onslaught of adversity" becomes "Wave of resilience." It transforms the image of overwhelming hardship into the surge of strength that rises to meet challenges, emphasizing the dynamic and powerful response to adversity.

488. "Onslaught of attacks" becomes "Onset of understanding." This shifts from an aggressive offensive to the beginning of mutual comprehension, emphasizing the importance of empathy in resolving disputes.

489. "Operation success" becomes "Mission of progress." Instead of a military operation's outcome, this phrase suggests a broader goal of advancing societal well-being, emphasizing the importance of continuous improvement.

490. "Operation victory" becomes "Mission of unity." This reframing moves from a military objective to a goal of bringing people together, highlighting the importance of solidarity and collective success.

491. "Orders to kill" becomes "Orders to protect." This reframing shifts the focus from taking lives to preserving them, emphasizing the responsibility to safeguard others and uphold the sanctity of life.

492. "Out of the ashes" becomes "Into the bloom." It transforms the image of destruction into one of growth and beauty, suggesting that from the remnants of the past, new life and opportunities can emerge.

493. "Out of the frying pan into the fire" becomes "From challenge to catalyst." This reframing suggests that moving from one difficult situation to another can serve as a powerful motivator for change and growth, rather than merely escalating

the problem.

494. "Outflanked by problems" becomes "Encircled by solutions." This reframing moves from being surrounded by difficulties to being enveloped by potential answers, highlighting the proactive search for and implementation of solutions.

495. "Outgunned and outnumbered" becomes "Leveraging unique strengths." It reframes a disadvantageous position into one where unique skills and abilities are recognized and utilized effectively.

496. "Outgunned" becomes "Outsmarted." Instead of focusing on the disparity in firepower, this phrase highlights the advantage of intelligence and strategy, promoting the value of wit over brute strength.

497. "Overcoming obstacles" becomes "Navigating pathways." It changes the narrative from battling barriers to discovering and following routes that lead to goals, emphasizing strategic thinking and adaptability.

498. "Overrun by the enemy" becomes "Overwhelmed by support." It changes the narrative from being dominated by adversaries to being surrounded by allies and support, promoting a sense of community and solidarity.

499. "Overwhelmed by chaos" becomes "Focused on clarity." It changes the narrative from being swamped by disorder to concentrating on finding clear, calm thoughts and solutions, emphasizing the power of maintaining focus amidst turmoil.

500. "Paralyzed by fear" becomes "Motivated by courage." Instead of being immobilized by anxiety, this phrase suggests being propelled forward by bravery, highlighting the transformative power of facing fears with determination.

501. "Pay the ultimate price" becomes "Champion the ultimate cause." By framing the cause as something to be actively championed, it encourages ongoing commitment and advocacy

rather than a finite endpoint.

502. "Paying the iron price" becomes "Investing in the golden future." This reframing moves from the concept of costly sacrifice to the idea of investing effort and resources into a prosperous and bright future for all.

503. "Peacekeeping forces" becomes "Peacebuilding communities." It shifts from the idea of imposing order to the concept of collectively creating a sustainable and inclusive peace, highlighting the role of community involvement in peace efforts.

504. "Perils of war" becomes "Paths to peace." Instead of focusing on the dangers of conflict, this phrase suggests the routes that lead away from violence towards peaceful resolutions, emphasizing the journey towards harmony.

505. "Picking up the pieces" becomes "Creating a mosaic." Instead of merely trying to put things back together, this reframing suggests forming something new and beautiful from the fragments, emphasizing creativity and reconstruction.

506. "Pitfalls of diplomacy" becomes "Stepping stones of negotiation." Instead of focusing on the risks and challenges in diplomatic efforts, this phrase suggests viewing them as opportunities for progress and understanding, emphasizing the constructive aspects of navigating complex discussions.

507. "Prepare for the worst" becomes "Hope for the best." This shifts the mindset from expecting negative outcomes to maintaining optimism for positive resolutions, fostering a climate of positivity and forward-thinking.

508. "Prisoners of circumstance" becomes "Navigators of destiny." It shifts from being controlled by external factors to actively steering one's course, emphasizing personal agency and the ability to influence outcomes.

509. "Prisoners of conflict" becomes "Liberators of potential." It transforms the concept of being trapped by disputes into the

role of freeing and realizing the possibilities for resolution and growth.

510. "Prisoners of war" becomes "Ambassadors of peace." This reframing suggests that those once held captive can become key figures in promoting peace, emphasizing the transformative roles individuals can play in reconciliation.

511. "Prisoners of war" becomes "Learners of peace." It shifts the focus from captivity to the opportunity for education and growth in peace-making, promoting the idea that even those most affected by conflict can become advocates for harmony.

512. "Psychological warfare" becomes "Psychological resilience." This reframing shifts from tactics designed to undermine and demoralize to strategies that build mental and emotional strength, promoting the development of coping mechanisms and inner fortitude.

513. "Pull the trigger" becomes "Press the button of dialogue." It changes the imagery from initiating violence to initiating conversation, highlighting the importance of communication in resolving disputes.

514. "Quagmire of despair" becomes "Meadow of aspiration." It shifts from a metaphorical swamp of hopelessness to a field of dreams and goals, emphasizing the potential for aspirations to thrive in open, nurturing environments.

515. "Quagmires of conflict" becomes "Meadows of cooperation." It transforms the imagery of being stuck in difficult disputes into open fields where collaborative efforts thrive, promoting the idea that working together leads to fruitful and peaceful outcomes.

516. "Quenched by pessimism" becomes "Sparked by possibility." Moving from extinguishing hope to igniting it with the potential for positive outcomes, this reframing promotes an optimistic view of the future.

517. "Quicksand of stagnation" becomes "Solid ground of progress." Instead of being trapped in inactivity, this phrase envisions a firm foundation that supports movement and advancement, emphasizing the importance of finding stable footing for growth.

518. "Rally the defenses" becomes "Rally the builders." Moving from preparing for an attack to gathering those who construct and create, this phrase promotes the idea of coming together to build rather than to defend.

519. "Rally the troops" becomes "Unite the community." This reframing suggests coming together not for battle but for collective action and support, emphasizing the strength found in unity.

520. "Rallying the troops" becomes "Gathering the community." Instead of preparing for battle, this phrase suggests bringing people together for support and collective action, emphasizing unity and communal strength.

521. "Rallying the war cry" becomes "Harmonizing the peace anthem." Instead of mobilizing for battle, this phrase encourages coming together in a chorus of peace, emphasizing the collective desire for harmony and understanding.

522. "Ravaged by conflict" becomes "Revived by unity." Instead of focusing on the damage caused by discord, this phrase emphasizes healing and strengthening through coming together, promoting collective recovery.

523. "Ravaged lands" becomes "Restored realms." This reframing shifts from the damage inflicted upon a place to the restoration and healing that can occur, promoting the idea of recovery and the return to a state of wholeness.

524. "Ravages of time" becomes "Patina of experience." This reframing moves from the negative effects of aging to the beauty and character that come with experience, promoting an

appreciation for the wisdom and depth gained over time.

525. "Ravages of war" becomes "Seeds of diplomacy." This reframing shifts from the damage caused by war to the beginnings of diplomatic efforts, emphasizing the potential for dialogue and negotiation to grow from conflict.

526. "Ravages of war" becomes "Seeds of peace." It transforms the focus from the destruction caused by conflict to the potential for cultivating peace in its aftermath, emphasizing that from devastation can come the opportunity for growth and harmony.

527. "Rebel without a cause" becomes "Innovator with a vision." It transforms the notion of aimless dissent into purposeful change-making, emphasizing the positive potential of challenging the status quo with clear intentions.

528. "Reconnaissance mission" becomes "Exploration journey." Instead of a military survey to gather information, this phrase suggests a voyage of curiosity and learning, promoting the idea of gaining knowledge through adventure.

529. "Retreating in defeat" becomes "Advancing with strategy." It shifts from withdrawal in the face of loss to moving forward with a plan, emphasizing the importance of learning from defeat to inform future actions.

530. "Rock bottom" becomes "Solid foundation." It shifts the perspective from despair to the potential for rebuilding, suggesting that the lowest points can provide a stable base upon which to construct a new beginning.

531. "Rubble of destruction" becomes "Foundation of construction." This reframing transforms the aftermath of devastation into the starting point for building anew, emphasizing the potential for positive change and renewal.

532. "Rubble of ruins" becomes "Bricks for building." It shifts from the debris of destruction to the materials for construction, promoting the idea that what is left behind can be used to create

something new and strong.

533. "Rubble of ruins" becomes "Foundation for the future." Instead of seeing destruction, this phrase envisions the remains as the base upon which to build anew, emphasizing the potential for growth and development from the aftermath.

534. "Rubble of the past" becomes "Foundation for the future." Instead of focusing on the remnants of destruction, this phrase envisions using the lessons and experiences of the past to build a stronger, more hopeful future.

535. "Ruins from battles" becomes "Foundations for peace." It transforms the imagery of destruction into the groundwork for harmony, promoting the idea that the aftermath of conflict can serve as a strong base for building a peaceful future.

536. "Ruins of conflict" becomes "Foundations for collaboration." It transforms the aftermath of discord into the groundwork for joint efforts, highlighting the potential to build strong partnerships on the lessons learned from past disputes.

537. "Ruins of the past" becomes "Edifice of the future." It shifts from the remains of what was to the construction of what will be, highlighting the potential to use past experiences as the foundation for future achievements.

538. "Ruins of the past" becomes "Foundations for the future." It transforms the narrative from destruction to the potential for building anew, emphasizing that the lessons learned from past conflicts can serve as a solid base for a peaceful and prosperous future.

539. "Ruins of the past" becomes "Foundations for tomorrow." Instead of dwelling on what has been destroyed, this phrase focuses on using the remnants as a base for future growth, emphasizing the potential to build anew on the lessons learned.

540. "Ruins of war" becomes "Blueprints for rebuilding." Instead of focusing on destruction, this phrase suggests seeing the

aftermath as a foundation for future construction, promoting the idea of growth and renewal from adversity.

541. "Ruins of war" becomes "Foundations for the future." Instead of focusing on destruction, this phrase envisions the remnants as the base upon which to build a new and hopeful future, emphasizing reconstruction and progress.

542. "Rules of engagement" becomes "Guidelines for harmony." This reframing moves from protocols for conflict to principles for peaceful coexistence, emphasizing the importance of guidelines that promote understanding and respect.

543. "Rules of engagement" becomes "Principles of cooperation." This reframing moves from guidelines for conflict to foundational ideas for working together, promoting the establishment of collaborative relationships.

544. "Sacrifice for the cause" becomes "Living for the cause." It redirects energy towards active and ongoing support for a cause, suggesting that one's efforts and passions can contribute to a cause without the need for self-sacrifice.

545. "Scars of battle" becomes "Marks of endurance." This reframing changes the narrative from wounds of war to symbols of the ability to withstand adversity, emphasizing the resilience and perseverance that challenges can foster.

546. "Scars of battle" becomes "Marks of honor." It changes the narrative from wounds and damage to symbols of bravery and survival, promoting the idea that overcoming adversity is a testament to strength and resilience.

547. "Scars of battle" becomes "Medals of honor." It changes the focus from the wounds of war to the recognition of bravery and experience, emphasizing the honor in enduring and the stories that scars can tell.

548. "Scars of conflict" becomes "Marks of courage." Instead of signs of suffering, this phrase suggests that scars can symbolize

resilience and bravery, highlighting the strength it takes to endure and overcome adversity.

549. "Scars of conflict" becomes "Medals of bravery." Instead of marks of pain, this phrase suggests symbols of courage and survival, highlighting the honor and recognition deserved for enduring hardship.

550. "Scars of division" becomes "Marks of unity." Instead of wounds that separate, this phrase envisions scars as symbols of coming together and healing, promoting the idea that overcoming division can lead to a stronger, more united community.

551. "Scars of the past" becomes "Lessons for the future." It changes the narrative from marks of pain to sources of wisdom, emphasizing the value of learning from history to inform better choices ahead.

552. "Scars of war" becomes "Badges of endurance." Instead of marks of violence, this phrase suggests symbols of the ability to withstand and persist, highlighting the resilience and strength that come from surviving adversity.

553. "Scorched battlefield" becomes "Nurtured landscape." Instead of a place marked by the ravages of war, this phrase envisions an area being cared for and restored, emphasizing the potential for healing and growth.

554. "Scorched by conflict" becomes "Refined by resolution." Instead of being damaged by disputes, this phrase suggests being improved and honed through the process of finding resolutions, emphasizing the refinement that comes with resolving issues.

555. "Scorched by flames" becomes "Refined by fire." Instead of focusing on the damage caused by fire, this phrase suggests the purifying and strengthening process it can represent, promoting the idea of emerging stronger from trials.

556. "Scorched earth policy" becomes "Green earth policy."

Instead of a strategy of destruction and denial of resources, this phrase suggests a commitment to environmental preservation and sustainability, highlighting proactive care for the planet.

557. "Scorched earth tactics" becomes "Green earth strategies." This reframing changes the narrative from destructive methods to sustainable practices, highlighting the importance of preserving and nurturing the environment.

558. "Scorched earth" becomes "Fertile ground." Instead of destruction that leaves nothing behind, this phrase suggests that from the ashes can come rich soil for new growth, emphasizing recovery and the promise of regeneration.

559. "Scorched earth" becomes "Fertile ground." It changes the narrative from destruction to potential for new growth, highlighting the opportunity to rebuild and renew after adversity.

560. "Scorched earth" becomes "Fertile soil." It transforms the image of barrenness into one of potential growth, suggesting that from destruction can come the conditions for new life to flourish.

561. "Seal one's fate" becomes "Seal one's commitment to life." This phrase emphasizes a binding dedication to living fully and meaningfully, promoting a life-affirming approach to decision-making.

562. "Shadow of death" becomes "Light of existence." This transformation moves the emphasis from looming mortality to the illumination of life, highlighting the brightness and potential that life offers.

563. "Shadowed by fear" becomes "Illuminated by courage." It shifts from being dominated by apprehension to being defined by bravery, highlighting the transformative power of facing fears with boldness.

564. "Shadows of conflict" becomes "Light of consensus." This reframing moves from the darkness cast by disagreement to the illumination that agreement brings, emphasizing the clarity and

unity achieved through finding common ground.

565. "Shadows of sorrow" becomes "Sunlight of joy." This reframing moves from the darkness cast by sadness to the brightness of happiness, promoting the idea that joy can emerge and shine even after the darkest times.

566. "Shadows of war" becomes "Light of reconciliation." Moving from the darkness cast by conflict to the illumination of coming together, this reframing promotes the healing and unifying power of seeking peace.

567. "Shattered dreams" becomes "Mosaic of possibilities." This reframing changes the narrative from broken aspirations to a beautiful, complex picture made of diverse opportunities, emphasizing the creative potential in reassembling hopes into new forms.

568. "Shattered dreams" becomes "Refashioned aspirations." Instead of focusing on what has been broken, this phrase suggests reshaping and adapting one's goals, emphasizing the flexibility and creativity in pursuing new paths.

569. "Shattered peace" becomes "Pieced together harmony." Moving from the idea of irreparable damage to a meticulous and careful restoration of calm, this reframing promotes the potential for creating a more resilient and inclusive peace.

570. "Shields of defense" becomes "Open arms of welcome." Instead of protective barriers, this phrase envisions a gesture of acceptance and inclusion, promoting the idea of safety and support through community rather than isolation.

571. "Shields up" becomes "Hands open." Moving from a defensive posture to one of welcome and generosity, this reframing promotes the idea of extending friendship and support rather than preparing for conflict.

572. "Shots fired" becomes "Hands shaken." This reframing moves from an act of aggression to a gesture of agreement and

partnership, promoting the value of making peace and forging alliances.

573. "<u>Siege mentality</u>" becomes "<u>Bridge-building mindset.</u>" Instead of a defensive and isolated outlook, this phrase suggests an open and connective approach, emphasizing the importance of reaching out and establishing connections.

574. "<u>Siege mentality</u>" becomes "<u>Community spirit.</u>" Instead of a defensive and isolated outlook, this phrase suggests a collective and inclusive approach, emphasizing the strength found in unity and shared purpose.

575. "<u>Siege mentality</u>" becomes "<u>Community spirit.</u>" Moving from a mindset of being under attack to one of collective strength and support, this phrase promotes the power of unity and mutual aid.

576. "<u>Siege mentality</u>" becomes "<u>Oasis mentality.</u>" Moving from a mindset of being under attack to one of finding or creating a peaceful refuge, this phrase promotes the idea of cultivating calm and tranquility amidst turmoil.

577. "<u>Siege mentality</u>" becomes "<u>Open arms approach.</u>" Moving from a defensive and closed mindset to one of welcome and openness, this phrase promotes inclusivity and the willingness to engage with others.

578. "<u>Siege mentality</u>" becomes "<u>Openness mindset.</u>" Moving from a defensive and closed attitude to one of receptivity and willingness to engage, this phrase promotes the benefits of dialogue and exchange over isolation.

579. "<u>Siege mentality</u>" becomes "<u>Sanctuary mindset.</u>" Instead of a defensive and fearful outlook, this phrase suggests a perspective of creating safe, welcoming spaces for all, emphasizing protection and inclusivity.

580. "<u>Siege mentality</u>" becomes "<u>Sanctuary mindset.</u>" Moving from a defensive and enclosed attitude to one of safety and

support, this phrase promotes the idea of creating spaces where people can find refuge and peace.

581. "Siege of negativity" becomes "Fortress of optimism." This reframing suggests transforming an environment overwhelmed by pessimism into a stronghold of positive thinking, emphasizing the protective and empowering nature of maintaining an optimistic outlook.

582. "Silenced forever" becomes "Echoing through eternity." Reframing death as an eternal echo suggests that one's words and deeds continue to resonate and influence long after they have passed.

583. "Sinking ship" becomes "Launching lifeboats." Instead of focusing on failure or disaster, this phrase emphasizes proactive rescue and survival strategies, highlighting hope and action in the face of adversity.

584. "Smoke of battle" becomes "Mist of renewal." It changes the imagery from the aftermath of conflict to the refreshing and cleansing aspect of mist, promoting the idea of purification and new beginnings.

585. "Soldier's farewell" becomes "Peacemaker's greeting." Instead of marking an end, this phrase signifies a beginning, focusing on the role of building peace and fostering connections rather than the separation of departure.

586. "Soldiers of fortune" becomes "Ambassadors of hope." This reframing moves from the notion of mercenary activity to the role of spreading optimism and possibility, emphasizing the positive impact individuals can have on the world.

587. "Sound the alarm" becomes "Ring the bell of harmony." It changes the call to arms into a call for accord, suggesting a summoning of efforts towards peaceful coexistence.

588. "Sound the battle cry" becomes "Sing the anthem of accord." Instead of a call to arms, this reframing is a call to unity,

suggesting a collective voice raised in agreement and cooperation.

589. "Stand one's ground" becomes "Share common ground." This phrase encourages finding and building upon areas of agreement, promoting collaboration over confrontation.

590. "Standoff at dawn" becomes "Concord at daybreak." It changes a tense confrontation at the start of the day to a harmonious agreement, symbolizing new beginnings and the promise of a peaceful day ahead.

591. "Staring down the barrel" becomes "Looking towards the horizon." It changes the imagery from facing imminent danger to gazing into the future, promoting a forward-thinking and optimistic outlook.

592. "Staring down the barrel" becomes "Looking up at the sky." By changing the focus from a confrontation with death to an observation of the vastness above, this phrase encourages a perspective of hope and the infinite possibilities that lie beyond current challenges.

593. "Staring into the abyss" becomes "Gazing at new horizons." This reframing moves from looking into a void to anticipating the vast possibilities that lie ahead, promoting a forward-looking and hopeful perspective.

594. "Stifled by limitations" becomes "Inspired by challenges." Instead of being suppressed by constraints, this phrase suggests being stimulated by the hurdles to be overcome, promoting a mindset that sees obstacles as opportunities for creativity.

595. "Storms of adversity" becomes "Winds of change." Instead of turbulent times that challenge us, this phrase envisions forces that propel us towards growth and transformation, promoting the idea that adversity can drive significant positive change.

596. "Storms of hatred" becomes "Showers of compassion." Instead of destructive forces driven by animosity, this phrase envisions nourishing rains that bring growth and healing,

emphasizing the transformative power of kindness and empathy.

597. "Storms of war" becomes "Breezes of reconciliation." Instead of turbulent times brought by conflict, this phrase envisions gentle winds leading to healing and coming together, promoting the gentle and steady process of reconciliation.

598. "Strategic position" becomes "Harmonious alignment." This reframing suggests not just a calculated placement for advantage but also a thoughtful arrangement that leads to balance and cooperation.

599. "Strategic withdrawal" becomes "Strategic advancement." Instead of retreating, this phrase suggests moving forward with a plan that benefits all parties involved, emphasizing the importance of strategic thinking for positive outcomes.

600. "Struggle for power" becomes "Collaboration for empowerment." It changes the narrative from competing for dominance to working together for mutual strengthening, highlighting the benefits of shared efforts and collective uplift.

601. "Succumbing to the inevitable" becomes "Rising to transcendence." Instead of surrendering to death, this phrase suggests an elevation to a higher state of being, implying a transformation or continuation of the spirit beyond physical existence.

602. "Surrender to death" becomes "Embrace the will to live." It encourages a strong desire to survive and thrive, fostering resilience and a determination to overcome adversity.

603. "Survival mode" becomes "Thrive mindset." Instead of merely getting by, this phrase emphasizes living with intention and seeking out pathways to flourish, focusing on the proactive pursuit of well-being.

604. "Survival mode" becomes "Thriving mode." It shifts from merely getting by to actively flourishing, promoting a mindset focused on growth, joy, and fulfillment beyond mere survival.

605. "Survival of the fittest" becomes "Thriving through collaboration." This reframing moves from a competitive struggle to a cooperative approach, emphasizing the benefits of working together for mutual success.

606. "Survive the onslaught" becomes "Thrive in cooperation." It reframes enduring an aggressive attack to flourishing through collaborative efforts, emphasizing mutual support and success.

607. "Surviving the odds" becomes "Thriving through challenges." It shifts from merely getting by in difficult circumstances to flourishing and finding opportunities for development, highlighting the proactive stance against adversity.

608. "Surviving the siege" becomes "Thriving beyond the siege." Instead of merely enduring an attack, this phrase suggests flourishing after adversity, highlighting the potential for positive development in the aftermath of challenges.

609. "Surviving the storm" becomes "Embracing the renewal." This suggests that after a storm comes a period of renewal and fresh starts, focusing on the positive aftermath and opportunities for rebuilding.

610. "Surviving the trenches" becomes "Thriving beyond barriers." It changes the narrative from merely enduring hardship to flourishing after overcoming obstacles, promoting a forward-looking perspective that focuses on growth and success.

611. "Survivors of conflict" becomes "Architects of the future." It transforms the identity from merely enduring hardship to actively shaping what comes next, highlighting the agency and creativity of those who have experienced war.

612. "Swan song" becomes "Dawn chorus." This transformation moves from a final performance to the promise of a new day filled with potential and the harmonious beginnings that each morning offers.

613. "Swept away by change" becomes "Riding the waves of innovation." Instead of being overwhelmed by transformation, this phrase suggests actively engaging with and utilizing change for creative and constructive purposes.

614. "Sword of Damocles" becomes "Olive branch of opportunity." Instead of a looming threat, this phrase suggests an offering of peace and the chance to transform a tense situation into a positive one.

615. "Swords into plowshares" becomes "Ideas into innovations." This classic reframing not only suggests transforming tools of war into tools of peace but also emphasizes turning concepts into creative solutions for the betterment of society.

616. "Tactical assault" becomes "Strategic embrace." Instead of an aggressive attack, this phrase promotes a considered and inclusive approach, emphasizing the power of embracing diverse strategies for the common good.

617. "Tactical maneuvers" becomes "Strategic partnerships." It changes the focus from military strategies to collaborative efforts, highlighting the importance of working together strategically for mutual benefit.

618. "Tactical retreat" becomes "Strategic advancement." Instead of backing down, this phrase suggests moving forward in a way that is thoughtful and purposeful, focusing on long-term goals and the bigger picture.

619. "Tactical retreat" becomes "Strategic advancement." It changes the narrative from withdrawal to progress, emphasizing that sometimes stepping back is part of a larger plan for moving forward more effectively.

620. "Tactical retreat" becomes "Strategic regrouping." This reframing moves from a notion of withdrawal to one of thoughtful reorganization, emphasizing the importance of

planning and preparation for future endeavors.

621. "Tactics of war" becomes "Strategies for peace." Instead of methods for conducting conflict, this phrase suggests approaches to achieving and maintaining peace, highlighting the importance of thoughtful, deliberate actions for harmony.

622. "Take up arms" becomes "Take up the cause of peace." This shifts from preparing for war to actively advocating for peace, highlighting a commitment to non-violence and resolution.

623. "Tattered remnants" becomes "Tapestries of resilience." This reframing moves from focusing on the worn pieces left behind to the beautiful, intricate work of art that life's experiences weave together, emphasizing the strength and beauty in the stories we create from our challenges.

624. "Tears of sorrow" becomes "Seeds of empathy." Instead of dwelling on grief, this phrase suggests that expressions of sadness can plant the beginnings of deeper understanding and connection among people, promoting emotional growth.

625. "The aftermath of war" becomes "The dawn of understanding." This reframing shifts from the consequences of conflict to the new beginnings that can emerge through mutual comprehension, highlighting the potential for peace and empathy to grow from adversity.

626. "The art of war" becomes "The art of reconciliation." It reframes the strategic approach to conflict into a creative approach to mending differences, emphasizing the skill and care involved in healing divisions.

627. "The battle rages on" becomes "The collaboration flourishes." It shifts from ongoing conflict to the thriving of cooperative efforts, emphasizing the positive dynamics of teamwork and joint problem-solving.

628. "The cessation of being" becomes "The transformation of essence." By reframing death as a transformation, it becomes

a process through which one's essence undergoes a profound change, suggesting continuity rather than termination.

629. "The closing of eyes" becomes "The opening of hearts." This phrase suggests that even as one's physical sight ends, the emotional and spiritual insight they've provided opens the hearts of those they've touched.

630. "The crosshairs of conflict" becomes "The meeting point of perspectives." This reframing turns a target in warfare into a place where different viewpoints converge, promoting the idea that from diversity can come greater understanding and unity.

631. "The die is cast" becomes "The path is chosen." This phrase suggests that rather than fate being sealed, there is a deliberate choice to follow a path of constructive action and positive outcomes.

632. "The drums of war" becomes "The symphony of accord." This phrase changes the call to arms into a harmonious blend of voices and ideas working in concert, symbolizing unity and mutual understanding.

633. "The eleventh hour" becomes "The first step." This reframing turns a last-minute crisis into the beginning of a journey, emphasizing the potential for positive action no matter the timing.

634. "The end of the line" becomes "The start of the journey." This reframing suggests that what may seem like a conclusion is actually the commencement of a new adventure, promoting optimism and the anticipation of future experiences.

635. "The end of the road" becomes "A new path unfolds." This reframing offers a sense of possibility and exploration, implying that even when one road ends, another begins, full of potential for positive change.

636. "The enemy at the gates" becomes "The friend at the door." It changes the perception of an imminent threat to the presence

of a potential ally, promoting an attitude of openness and friendship.

637. "The enemy within" becomes "The ally within." It shifts from identifying internal conflict to recognizing inner strength and support, promoting self-compassion and the recognition of one's own capacity for resilience.

638. "The extinguishing of the flame" becomes "The spreading of warmth." Instead of focusing on the end of life as an extinguishing, this reframing highlights the warmth and light one has contributed to the world, which continues to spread even after they're gone.

639. "The final blow" becomes "The final stand for peace." It implies a commitment to making a lasting impact for peace, suggesting that the ultimate goal is not to end in conflict but to establish a legacy of harmony.

640. "The final chapter" becomes "The legacy we write." This reframing encourages us to view life as a story where the final chapter is an opportunity to solidify one's legacy and the lasting impressions we leave behind.

641. "The final curtain" becomes "The opening act." By reframing the end as a beginning, this phrase suggests that every conclusion is also the start of something new, encouraging a view of life as a series of opportunities and renewals.

642. "The fog of uncertainty" becomes "The clarity of purpose." Instead of being paralyzed by doubt, this phrase suggests finding direction and intentionality, emphasizing the power of having a clear goal in navigating life's challenges.

643. "The fog of war" becomes "The clarity of compassion." This reframing shifts from the confusion of conflict to the lucidity brought by empathy, promoting the idea that understanding and caring for others can guide us through turmoil.

644. "The fog of war" becomes "The clarity of consensus."

Shifting from confusion and uncertainty to clear agreement, this reframing emphasizes the power of reaching a mutual understanding and shared vision.

645. "The fog of war" becomes "The clarity of dialogue." This reframing moves away from confusion and uncertainty towards clear, open communication as a means to resolve conflict.

646. "The fog of war" becomes "The clarity of peace." It shifts from the confusion and uncertainty of conflict to the transparency and understanding that peace brings, highlighting the benefits of clear communication and mutual comprehension.

647. "The great unknown" becomes "The great adventure." By reframing death as an adventure, it becomes less about fear and uncertainty and more about curiosity and the potential for discovery, much like embarking on an uncharted expedition.

648. "The killing fields" becomes "The healing gardens." It transforms a place of death into a place of restoration and growth, focusing on the healing power of nature and the human spirit.

649. "The point of no return" becomes "The moment of new beginnings." This reframing turns a moment of irreversible decision into an opportunity for fresh starts and new ventures, focusing on the future rather than the past.

650. "The silence of isolation" becomes "The quiet of reflection." It changes the narrative from loneliness to a peaceful solitude that allows for introspection and self-discovery, highlighting the value of quiet moments.

651. "The spoils of war" becomes "The rewards of reconciliation." Instead of gains obtained through conflict, this phrase highlights the benefits that come from mending differences and building bridges, focusing on the positive outcomes of peace efforts.

652. "The stillness of the grave" becomes "The peace of fulfillment." Instead of associating the grave with stillness and

inactivity, this phrase reframes it as a place of peace, signifying a life lived to its fullest and now at rest.

653. "The void of absence" becomes "The space for remembrance." This reframing turns the emptiness left by a loss into a sacred space for honoring and remembering the departed, emphasizing the importance of memory in keeping their spirit alive.

654. "Theater of operations" becomes "Arena of solutions." It changes the military term for a region where operations are conducted to a place where creative and effective solutions are sought and implemented.

655. "Theater of operations" becomes "Stage for cooperation." It changes a military term for areas of engagement into a platform for collaborative efforts, highlighting the potential for joint initiatives and teamwork.

656. "Theater of war" becomes "Stage of diplomacy." It changes the setting from one of conflict to one of negotiation and peaceful resolution, emphasizing the importance of dialogue and understanding in resolving disputes.

657. "Theatre of war" becomes "Stage of diplomacy." Instead of a setting for conflict, this phrase suggests a platform for negotiation and peaceful resolution, promoting the arts of diplomacy and statesmanship.

658. "Theatre of war" becomes "Stage of peace." This reframing changes a setting of conflict into a platform for peacebuilding activities, emphasizing the role of deliberate, constructive actions in creating harmony.

659. "This is a good day to die" becomes "This is a good day to cherish life." This positive outlook reminds us to appreciate the present and the potential for joy, fostering an environment where life is celebrated over the acceptance of death.

660. "This is the hill we die on" becomes "This is the hill

we protect for life." Reframing to protection rather than death emphasizes the value of safeguarding what is cherished, encouraging a mindset focused on preservation and the future.

661. "Thrown to the wolves" becomes "Joining the pack." Instead of abandonment or betrayal, this phrase suggests finding strength and camaraderie in unexpected places, highlighting resilience and adaptability.

662. "Thunder of cannons" becomes "Whispers of calm." It changes the narrative from the loud, disruptive sounds of warfare to the soft, soothing sounds of tranquility, highlighting the contrast between conflict and peace.

663. "Tides of turmoil" becomes "Currents of change." It transforms the imagery from chaotic, uncontrollable waves to directed flows that signify progress, highlighting the opportunities for positive transformation amidst upheaval.

664. "To fall in battle" becomes "To rise for peace." This phrase suggests an elevation above conflict, advocating for efforts that build towards reconciliation and the cessation of hostilities.

665. "To perish in conflict" becomes "To prevail in unity." It suggests that success is found in coming together and finding common ground, highlighting the power of collective action in overcoming division.

666. "Toll of battle" becomes "Investment in peace." This reframing suggests that the costs incurred from conflict are not just losses but also investments in the pursuit of lasting peace, highlighting the long-term benefits of working towards harmony.

667. "Toll of conflict" becomes "Investment in resolution." This reframing suggests that the costs incurred from disputes are not just losses but contributions towards achieving peace and understanding, highlighting the value of working towards reconciliation.

668. "Torn apart by war" becomes "Woven together by peace."

It shifts from the narrative of division and destruction to one of reconciliation and building a cohesive community, highlighting the constructive power of peace efforts.

669. "Torn asunder" becomes "Woven together." It shifts from the imagery of being ripped apart to the act of interlacing threads into a stronger fabric, emphasizing the unity and strength that can come from repairing what was once broken.

670. "Trapped by circumstances" becomes "Freed by choices." This reframing moves from a sense of entrapment by situations to an empowerment through decision-making, highlighting the agency one has in navigating and altering their path.

671. "Trapped in conflict" becomes "Exploring paths to peace." It shifts from a feeling of entrapment to an exploration of options, emphasizing the journey towards peaceful resolutions.

672. "Trapped in turmoil" becomes "Free in forgiveness." It changes the narrative from being confined by unrest to finding liberation through the act of forgiving, promoting the freedom that comes with letting go of grudges.

673. "Treading on thin ice" becomes "Walking on solid ground." It suggests moving from a precarious position to one of stability and certainty, emphasizing the importance of building a strong foundation for resolution.

674. "Treading water" becomes "Riding the waves." It shifts from a struggle to stay afloat to skillfully navigating challenges, emphasizing agility and the ability to use circumstances to one's advantage.

675. "Trench warfare" becomes "Bridge building." Instead of entrenched positions in prolonged conflict, this phrase suggests constructing connections and pathways to facilitate communication and reconciliation.

676. "Trench warfare" becomes "Bridge building." It shifts from a static and defensive form of combat to the active construction of

connections and understanding, promoting efforts to overcome divisions.

677. "Trench warfare" becomes "Bridge building." It shifts from entrenched positions and stalemates to the construction of connections between sides, highlighting efforts to overcome division and foster collaboration.

678. "Trench warfare" becomes "Garden cultivation." This reframing transforms the concept of entrenched combat into the nurturing and growth of a garden, emphasizing creation and care over destruction.

679. "Trenches of despair" becomes "Gardens of hope." This reframing moves from the depths of hopelessness to cultivating spaces where optimism can grow and flourish, emphasizing the nurturing and life-affirming aspects of hope.

680. "Trenches of despair" becomes "Valleys of hope." This reframing suggests that even the lowest points can be places where hope flourishes, emphasizing the potential for positive change and the persistence of optimism.

681. "Trenches of despair" becomes "Valleys of vision." This reframing changes the narrative from being stuck in low points to seeing them as places from which one can look up and envision a better future, emphasizing hope and perspective.

682. "Trenches of distrust" becomes "Bridges of trust." This reframing moves from deep-seated suspicion to the construction of connections based on reliability and faith in one another, emphasizing the foundational role of trust in healing and cooperation.

683. "Trenches of division" becomes "Bridges of connection." Instead of deepening separations, this phrase suggests building structures that span divides, emphasizing efforts to connect and understand each other across differences.

684. "Trenches of division" becomes "Bridges of connection."

This reframing transforms symbols of separation into structures that facilitate unity, emphasizing efforts to overcome differences and foster understanding.

685. "Trenches of division" becomes "Plains of unity." It shifts from deep separations to vast, open lands of togetherness, highlighting the expansive opportunities for connection and solidarity across previously divided lines.

686. "Trojan horse" becomes "Gift of trust." Instead of a deceptive strategy, this phrase suggests an offering that builds confidence and friendship, promoting the value of sincerity and open-heartedness.

687. "Trojan horse" becomes "Olive branch." Instead of a deceptive threat, this phrase suggests a genuine offer of peace, highlighting sincerity and the desire for reconciliation.

688. "Under attack" becomes "Open to engagement." Instead of a stance of victimhood, this phrase promotes a readiness to engage with others, suggesting a proactive and open-minded approach to conflict.

689. "Under pressure" becomes "In the forge of character." It shifts from the stress of demands to the idea of being shaped and strengthened by them, emphasizing personal development and fortitude.

690. "Under siege" becomes "Embracing resilience." This reframing moves from a scenario of being attacked and trapped to recognizing and harnessing the inner strength and adaptability that challenging situations can foster, emphasizing growth through adversity.

691. "Under siege" becomes "Embracing sanctuary." This reframing suggests finding refuge and safety, rather than being trapped and isolated, promoting the idea of protection and community support.

692. "Under the gun" becomes "Under the banner of peace."

This phrase changes the pressure of an imminent threat to the protection and unity under a shared commitment to peace.

693. "Up in arms" becomes "Hand in hand." This reframing moves from conflict and readiness to fight to unity and cooperation, promoting peace and collective effort.

694. "Veil of tears" becomes "Canvas of joy." This reframing shifts from a perspective of sorrow to one of happiness and potential, emphasizing the ability to paint one's life with moments of joy despite past sorrows.

695. "Veterans of war" becomes "Champions of peace." Instead of focusing solely on their combat roles, this phrase highlights the potential for veterans to lead in peace-building efforts, recognizing their experience and dedication to service.

696. "Victims of conflict" becomes "Architects of peace." This reframing recognizes that those affected by the conflict have the power to shape a peaceful future. It emphasizes the agency of individuals and communities in building bridges and crafting solutions that lead to lasting harmony.

697. "Volcanoes of anger" becomes "Mountains of resolve." It transforms the destructive potential of rage into the majestic and steadfast determination, promoting the idea that strong emotions can be channeled into powerful commitments to action and change.

698. "Wading through bloodshed" becomes "Walking towards healing." This reframing suggests moving away from the aftermath of violence to a journey of collective healing and restoration, emphasizing the communal effort to mend and recover.

699. "Waging war" becomes "Cultivating peace." It reframes the active pursuit of conflict into the active fostering of peaceful relations, emphasizing constructive actions over destructive ones.

700. "Walking into the valley of death" becomes "Walking into

the valley of life." Reframing in this way changes a journey marked by peril into one filled with possibilities and growth, suggesting a path that leads to flourishing landscapes rather than desolation.

701. "Walking on a battlefield" becomes "Navigating a landscape of opportunities." This reframing turns a dangerous terrain into a land rich with possibilities, encouraging a perspective that looks for chances to grow and succeed.

702. "Walking on eggshells" becomes "Dancing on air." Instead of cautious and fearful interaction, this phrase suggests moving through life with joy and ease, emphasizing the liberation from anxiety and the embrace of positive dynamics.

703. "Walking through fire" becomes "Illuminated by flames." Instead of enduring pain and danger, this reframing suggests being enlightened and guided by the experience, promoting the idea that challenges can shed light on our path and reveal our strength.

704. "Walls of resistance" becomes "Doors of opportunity." It changes the narrative from barriers that block progress to gateways that open to new possibilities, promoting the idea that overcoming resistance can lead to unexpected and rewarding paths.

705. "Walls of separation" becomes "Windows of opportunity." It shifts from barriers that divide to openings that invite exploration and connection, emphasizing the potential for new experiences and relationships.

706. "Walls of separation" becomes "Windows to understanding." It transforms barriers into opportunities for insight into each other's perspectives, highlighting the importance of empathy and the potential for increased closeness through shared knowledge.

707. "War games" becomes "Peace simulations." This reframing

moves from practice for conflict to rehearsal for peace, emphasizing the value of preparing and planning for peaceful interactions and resolutions.

708. "War of attrition" becomes "Endurance of spirit." Instead of a prolonged struggle to wear down the opposition, this phrase highlights the resilience and perseverance of the human spirit, promoting the idea of inner strength.

709. "War of attrition" becomes "Peace of persistence." It changes the narrative from a prolonged struggle to deplete the enemy to a sustained effort to maintain and promote peace, highlighting the enduring commitment to harmony.

710. "War of words" becomes "Dialogue of discovery." Shifting from verbal conflict to exploratory conversation, this phrase emphasizes the value of learning and understanding through dialogue.

711. "War room" becomes "Peace hub." It transforms the concept of a place for planning military operations into a center for coordinating efforts to maintain and promote peace, highlighting the proactive work done to prevent conflict.

712. "War zone" becomes "Peace park." Instead of an area characterized by violence, this phrase envisions a space dedicated to tranquility and reflection, emphasizing the transformation of conflict areas into symbols of reconciliation.

713. "Warpath" becomes "Pathway to peace." Instead of a route leading to conflict, this phrase envisions a path directed towards reconciliation and harmony, promoting the journey towards peaceful relations.

714. "Warrior's armor" becomes "Healer's hands." This reframing shifts from the protection used in battle to the nurturing touch of someone who heals, emphasizing care, recovery, and the human capacity to mend and soothe.

715. "Warrior's armor" becomes "Peacemaker's embrace." This

reframing moves from the imagery of battle readiness to the warmth of inclusivity and acceptance, emphasizing compassion and unity over division.

716. "Warrior's cry" becomes "Healer's whisper." This reframing moves from a battle shout to the gentle voice of someone who heals, emphasizing the power of quiet support and the role of care in mending wounds and fostering peace.

717. "Warrior's path" becomes "Peacemaker's journey." It shifts from a trajectory marked by combat to one characterized by the pursuit of peace, highlighting the noble and ongoing effort to create harmony and understanding.

718. "Warrior's path" becomes "Peacemaker's way." Instead of a journey marked by combat, this phrase envisions a route defined by the pursuit of peace, highlighting the noble goal of resolving conflicts and fostering harmony.

719. "Warrior's spirit" becomes "Peacemaker's passion." It emphasizes channeling one's inner strength and courage into the pursuit of peace, rather than the waging of war, highlighting the fervor for creating harmony.

720. "Warrior's stance" becomes "Peacemaker's embrace." Instead of preparing for battle, this phrase envisions an approach of reconciliation and healing, emphasizing the role of peace efforts in resolving conflicts.

721. "Wartime" becomes "Peacetime." Instead of a period characterized by conflict, this phrase suggests a time filled with tranquility and harmony, promoting the idea that peace should be the norm rather than the exception.

722. "War-torn landscape" becomes "Canvas for creation." Instead of a backdrop marred by conflict, this phrase suggests a blank slate ready for new and constructive endeavors, highlighting the potential for creativity and rebuilding.

723. "War-torn regions" becomes "Recovery-rich regions."

Instead of focusing on the damage inflicted by conflict, this phrase highlights areas with a strong potential for healing and rebuilding, promoting a focus on resilience and restoration.

724. "War-torn societies" becomes "Rebuilding communities." Instead of dwelling on the destruction caused by conflict, this phrase focuses on the collective efforts to rebuild and heal, emphasizing the resilience of communities and the shared goal of restoring peace and prosperity.

725. "War-torn" becomes "Peace-bound." It changes the focus from the scars of conflict to the commitment to achieving peace, emphasizing the journey towards harmony and the collective aspiration for a tranquil future.

726. "War-torn" becomes "Peace-mended." Instead of focusing on the scars left by conflict, this phrase highlights the healing and unification that can occur, emphasizing the restorative power of peace efforts.

727. "War-torn" becomes "Peace-sewn." Instead of focusing on the scars of conflict, this phrase envisions the careful stitching together of a peaceful future, emphasizing healing and the deliberate crafting of harmony.

728. "War-torn" becomes "Peace-woven." Instead of focusing on the damage inflicted by conflict, this phrase emphasizes the intricate and deliberate process of crafting peace, highlighting the active creation of harmony.

729. "War-torn" becomes "Peace-woven." This shifts the narrative from the destruction of war to the fabric of peace being woven together, emphasizing restoration and the collective effort to create a cohesive community.

730. "Wasteland of conflict" becomes "Garden of collaboration." Instead of an area devastated by disagreement, this phrase envisions a fertile ground for cooperative efforts and joint success, promoting the growth of partnerships and shared achievements.

731. "Wasteland of conflict" becomes "Meadow of concord." Instead of an area devastated by disagreement, this phrase suggests a peaceful and fertile ground for agreement and mutual understanding, promoting the growth of peaceful relations.

732. "Wasteland of despair" becomes "Landscape of hope." It changes the narrative from a place devoid of hope to an area ripe with potential for optimism, emphasizing the possibility of transformation and the emergence of positive prospects.

733. "Wasteland of indifference" becomes "Garden of engagement." It transforms an area devoid of concern into a fertile space for active participation and interest, highlighting the growth that comes from caring involvement.

734. "Weapons at the ready" becomes "Ideas at the ready." Instead of preparing instruments of war, this phrase encourages the preparation of innovative thoughts and solutions, emphasizing intellectual readiness for problem-solving.

735. "Weapons of destruction" becomes "Instruments of creation." It transforms tools used for harm into those used for building and nurturing, emphasizing the potential to repurpose energies towards constructive and life-affirming activities.

736. "Weapons of destruction" becomes "Tools of construction." It transforms the concept of instruments used to harm into those used to build and create, promoting the positive potential of repurposing resources for the betterment of society.

737. "Weapons of destruction" becomes "Tools of creation." This reframing shifts from instruments that cause harm to those that build and innovate, emphasizing the positive potential of resources when directed towards constructive ends.

738. "Weapons of hostility" becomes "Instruments of harmony." This reframing changes tools used for aggression into those that create accord, emphasizing the choice to promote peace over perpetuating conflict.

739. "Weapons of hostility" becomes "Tools of understanding." It shifts from instruments of aggression to means of gaining insight and empathy, highlighting the importance of using our resources to foster connection rather than division.

740. "Weapons of mass destruction" becomes "Instruments of mass construction." It changes tools designed for harm into tools for building and creating, promoting the positive potential of technology and innovation for societal benefit.

741. "Weapons of mass destruction" becomes "Instruments of mass construction." It changes the focus from tools designed to harm to those intended to build and create, promoting the positive potential of repurposing resources for the betterment of society.

742. "Weapons of mass destruction" becomes "Tools of mass construction." This reframing changes the focus from instruments designed to harm to those intended to build and repair, promoting the positive potential of repurposing energies towards constructive ends.

743. "Weapons of war" becomes "Instruments of harmony." It transforms the tools used for fighting into those used for creating unity and accord, emphasizing the repurposing of energies towards constructive and unifying endeavors.

744. "Weapons of war" becomes "Instruments of peace." This reframing moves from tools designed for harm to those crafted for creating harmony, highlighting the potential to repurpose efforts towards constructive ends.

745. "Weathering the storm" becomes "Embracing the rainbow." This reframing suggests that instead of merely enduring hard times, one looks forward to the beauty and opportunities that follow adversity, symbolizing hope and renewal.

746. "Winning the battle" becomes "Achieving harmony." This reframing moves the focus from victory in conflict to the

accomplishment of balance and peace, highlighting the ultimate goal of conflict resolution.

747. "Withstanding the siege" becomes "Cultivating resilience." It changes the narrative from enduring a prolonged assault to actively developing the capacity to withstand and overcome adversity, highlighting personal growth and fortitude.

748. "Wounded by conflict" becomes "Healed through compassion." It shifts from focusing on the injuries inflicted by disputes to the healing that comes from empathy and understanding, emphasizing the restorative power of compassionate connections.

749. "Wounded in action" becomes "Healed through compassion." Shifting the focus from the injuries of conflict to the healing that comes from care and empathy, this phrase underscores the importance of support and understanding in recovery.

750. "Wounded pride" becomes "Strengthened character." It shifts from the hurt caused by damaged ego to the fortification of one's inner self, emphasizing the growth and maturity that can result from overcoming personal setbacks.

751. "Wounded soldiers" becomes "Healing heroes." It shifts from the pain and injury of conflict to the journey towards recovery, highlighting the courage it takes to heal and the inspiration these individuals provide as they overcome adversity.

752. "Wounded warriors" becomes "Healing heroes." Instead of focusing on the injuries sustained in conflict, this phrase emphasizes the journey towards recovery and the valor in overcoming adversity, promoting a narrative of resilience and courage.

753. "Wounds of conflict" becomes "Scars of strength." It transforms the narrative from focusing on the pain inflicted by adversity to recognizing the enduring marks as symbols of

resilience and survival, emphasizing the growth and fortitude that come from healing.

754. "Wounds of war" becomes "Wisdom of peace." This reframing moves from focusing on the injuries inflicted by conflict to the insights gained in the pursuit of peace, emphasizing the knowledge and understanding that come from striving for harmony.

755. "Wrestling with fate" becomes "Dancing with possibilities." This reframing moves from a struggle against destiny to an embrace of potential futures, emphasizing agency and the joy of exploring what could be.

756. "Yielding to darkness" becomes "Welcoming the dawn." Rather than succumbing to darkness, this phrase suggests the anticipation of a new beginning, akin to the hope and renewal that comes with the break of dawn.

757. "Zero ground" becomes "Common soil." Instead of a place of devastation, this phrase suggests fertile ground for new growth, emphasizing the shared foundation from which to cultivate new beginnings.

758. "Zero tolerance" becomes "Unlimited understanding." Instead of an inflexible approach, this phrase suggests an open-minded and empathetic stance, promoting the importance of compassion and comprehension.

759. "Zero-sum game" becomes "Win-win collaboration." This shifts from a perspective where one side's gain is another's loss to a cooperative approach where all parties can benefit.

760. "Zone of war" becomes "Area of healing." It transforms the concept of a region marked by conflict into a space dedicated to recovery and renewal, emphasizing the potential for areas and people affected by war to heal and rebuild.

www.ingramcontent.com/pod-product-compliance
Lightning Source LLC
Chambersburg PA
CBHW050314230526
45471CB00005B/2183